THE
Low Fat
Low Cholesterol
COOKBOOK

CHRISTINE FRANCE

THE
Low Fat
Low Cholesterol
COOKBOOK

CHRISTINE FRANCE

Over 130 healthy recipes – step-by-step

Photography by Karl Adamson

SMITHMARK

This edition published in 1994
by SMITHMARK Publishers Inc.
16 East 32nd Street
New York
NY 10016
USA

SMITHMARK books are available for bulk purchase for sales and
promotion and premium use. For details write or call the manager of
special sales,
SMITHMARK Publishers Inc.
16 East 32nd Street
New York
NY 100016
(212) 532-6600

Editorial Director: Joanna Lorenz
Series Editor: Linda Fraser
Copy Editor: Penny David
Designers: Tony Paine and Roy Prescott
Photographer: Karl Adamson
Food for Photography: Jane Stevenson
Props Stylist: Kirsty Rawlings

Printed and bound in Singapore

CONTENTS

WHY A LOW FAT DIET?

We need a certain amount of fat in our diet for general health and it is a valuable source of energy. Also, it plays a vital role in making foods palatable to eat. However, most of us eat more fat than we need. You should not try to cut out fat altogether, but a lower fat diet has the benefits of weight loss and reduction in the risk of heart disease.

There are two types of fat – saturated and unsaturated. The unsaturated group includes two types – polyunsaturated and monounsaturated fats.

Saturated fats are the ones you should limit, as they increase cholesterol in the blood, and this can increase the risk of heart disease. The main sources of saturated fat are animal products such as dairy products and meat, but also hard fats and hydrogenated vegetable fat or oil.

Polyunsaturated fats are essential in small quantities for good health, and are thought to help reduce the cholesterol in the blood. There is also some evidence that monounsaturated fats have a beneficial effect. The main sources of polyunsaturates are vegetable oils such as sunflower, corn and soybean, and oily fish such as herring, mackerel, sardines, and trout. Sources of monounsaturated fats include olive and peanut oils, as well as avocados and many nuts.

Cutting Down on Cholesterol?
Cholesterol is a substance which occurs naturally in the blood, and is essential for the formation of hormones, body cells, nerves, and bile salts which help digestion.

A high cholesterol level can increase the likelihood of coronary heart disease, as it becomes deposited on the walls of the arteries, causing them to fur up. The main cause of raised cholesterol levels is eating too much fat, especially saturated fat. Eating too much saturated fat encourages the body to make more cholesterol than it needs, and also seems to prevent it getting rid of the excess.

The cholesterol found in foods such as egg yolk, liver, cheese, butter, and shellfish does not have a major effect on the amount of blood cholesterol in most people, but it is best not to eat large quantities of these foods too often.

Fresh approach: when you are shopping for low fat foods, choose fresh seasonal vegetables (top right) and cook them without added fat. Salads (right) are a good accompaniment too, just use a polyunsaturated or monounsaturated oil for the dressing. Fresh fruits (above) are the perfect ending to a low fat meal if you haven't time to cook – eat them either raw in a salad or poach in fruit juice and serve hot with yogurt.

EASY WAYS TO CUT DOWN FAT AND SATURATED FAT

EAT LESS	TRY INSTEAD
Butter and hard fats.	Try spreading butter more thinly, or replace it with a low fat spread or polyunsaturated margarine.
Fatty meats and high-fat products such as meat dishes in heavy sauces and sausages.	Buy the leanest cuts of meat you can find and choose low fat meats like skinless chicken or turkey. Look for reduced-fat sausages and meat products. Eat fish more often, especially oily fish.
Full-fat dairy products like cream, butter, yogurt, milk, and hard cheeses.	Choose skimmed or semi-skimmed milk and milk products, and try low fat yogurt, low fat fromage frais, and lower fat cheeses such as skim milk cream cheese, reduced fat Cheddar, mozzarella, or Brie.
Cooking fats such as lard or shortening.	Choose polyunsaturated oils for cooking, such as olive, sunflower, corn, or soybean oil.
Rich salad dressings like Blue Cheese or Thousand Island.	Make salad dressings with low fat yogurt or fromage frais, or use a healthy oil such as olive oil.
Fried foods.	Broil, microwave, steam, or bake when possible. Roast meats on a rack. Fill up on starchy foods like pasta, rice, and couscous. Choose baked or boiled potatoes, not fries.
Added fat in cooking.	Use heavy-based or nonstick pans so you can cook with little or no added fat.
High fat snacks such as chips, chocolate, cakes, pastries, and cookies.	Choose fresh or dried fruit, breadsticks, or vegetable sticks. Make your own low fat cakes and baked goods.

APPETIZERS AND SNACKS

For a healthy diet it makes good sense to include some home-made soups in everyday meals, packed with the goodness of fresh ingredients and very low in fat. As a light lunch with crusty bread, or as an appetizer, modern soups are extremely quick and easy to make. The Thai-style Corn Soup takes only two to three minutes. An added bonus is the variety of fresh, seasonal vegetables available all year. Other appetizers can double up as a light meal or snack. It pays to have a selection of these healthy, quick snack foods handy. For simple snacks or lunch boxes, pitas, whole-wheat rolls, or tacos can contain a tasty, low fat filling like chili-spiced tuna salad. Some snacks are elegant enough for dinner party appetizers too.

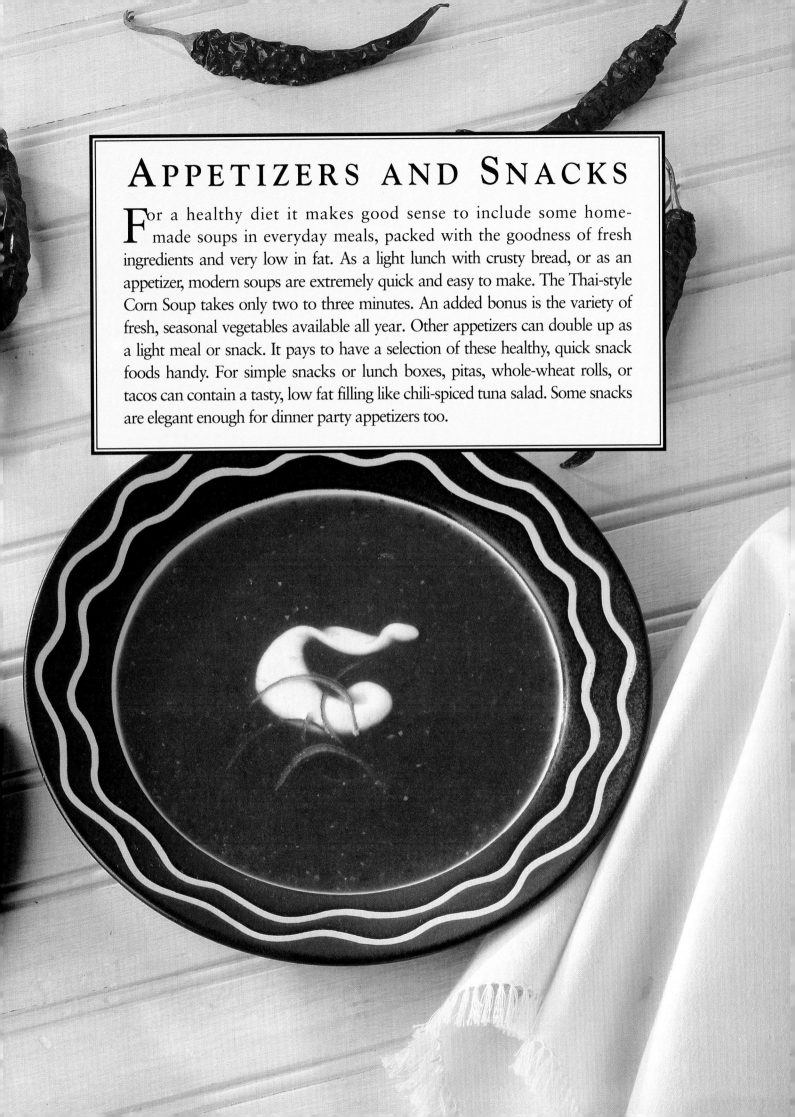

SPLIT PEA AND ZUCCHINI SOUP

Rich and satisfying, this tasty and nutritious soup will warm a chilly winter's day.

INGREDIENTS

Serves 4

1⅞ *cups yellow split peas*
1 *medium onion, finely chopped*
1 *tsp sunflower oil*
2 *medium zucchini, finely diced*
3¾ *cups chicken broth*
½ *tsp ground turmeric*
salt and black pepper

1 Place the split peas in a bowl, cover with cold water, and leave to soak for several hours or overnight. Drain, rinse in cold water, and drain again.

2 Cook the onion in the oil in a covered pan, shaking occasionally, until soft. Reserve a handful of diced zucchini and add the rest to the pan. Cook, stirring, for 2–3 minutes.

3 Add the broth and turmeric to the pan and bring to a boil. Reduce the heat, then cover and simmer for 30–40 minutes, or until the split peas are tender. Adjust the seasoning.

4 When the soup is almost ready, bring a large saucepan of water to a boil, add the reserved diced zucchini, and cook for 1 minute, then drain and add to the soup before serving hot with warm crusty bread.

COOK'S TIP
For a quicker alternative, use split red lentils for this soup – they need no pre-soaking and cook very quickly. Adjust the amount of broth, if necessary.

NUTRITION NOTES

Per portion:

Energy	174Kcals/730kJ
Fat	2.14g
Saturated fat	0.54g
Cholesterol	0
Fiber	3.43g

RED BELL PEPPER SOUP WITH LIME

The beautiful rich red color of this soup makes it a very attractive appetizer or light lunch. For a special dinner, toast some tiny croutons and serve sprinkled into the soup.

INGREDIENTS

Serves 4–6
4 red bell peppers, seeded and chopped
1 large onion, chopped
1 tsp olive oil
1 garlic clove, crushed
1 small red chili, sliced
3 tbsp tomato paste
3¾ cups chicken broth
finely grated rind and juice of 1 lime
salt and black pepper
shreds of lime rind, to garnish

1 Cook the onion and bell peppers gently in the oil in a covered saucepan for about 5 minutes, shaking the pan occasionally, until softened.

2 Stir in the garlic, then add the chili with the tomato paste. Stir in half the broth, then bring to a boil. Cover the pan and simmer for 10 minutes.

3 Cool slightly, then purée in a food processor or blender. Return to the pan, then add the remaining broth, the lime rind and juice, and seasoning.

4 Bring the soup back to a boil, then serve at once with a few strips of lime rind, scattered into each bowl.

NUTRITION NOTES

Per portion:	
Energy	87Kcals/366kJ
Fat	1.57g
Saturated fat	0.12g
Cholesterol	0
Fiber	3.40g

CAULIFLOWER AND WALNUT CREAM

Even though there's no cream added to this soup, the cauliflower gives it a delicious, rich, creamy texture.

INGREDIENTS

Serves 4

1 medium cauliflower
1 medium onion, coarsely chopped
1⅞ cups chicken or vegetable broth
1⅞ cups skim milk
3 tbsp walnut pieces
salt and black pepper
paprika and chopped walnuts, to garnish

1 Trim the cauliflower of outer leaves and break into small florets. Place the cauliflower, onion, and broth in a large saucepan.

2 Bring to a boil, cover, and simmer for about 15 minutes, or until soft. Add the milk and walnuts, then purée in a food processor until smooth.

3 Season the soup to taste, then bring to a boil. Serve sprinkled with paprika and chopped walnuts.

NUTRITION NOTES	
Per portion:	
Energy	166Kcals/699kJ
Fat	9.02g
Saturated fat	0.88g
Cholesterol	2.25mg
Fiber	2.73g

CURRIED CARROT AND APPLE SOUP

INGREDIENTS

Serves 4

2 tsp sunflower oil
1 tbsp mild curry powder
1¼ lb carrots, chopped
1 large onion, chopped
1 tart baking apple, chopped
3⅔ cups chicken broth
salt and black pepper
plain low fat yogurt and carrot curls, to garnish

NUTRITION NOTES	
Per portion:	
Energy	114Kcals/477kJ
Fat	3.57g
Saturated fat	**0.43g**
Cholesterol	**0.4mg**
Fiber	**4.99g**

1 Heat the oil and gently fry the curry powder for 2–3 minutes.

2 Add the carrots, onion, and apple, stir well, then cover the pan.

3 Cook over very low heat for about 15 minutes, shaking the pan occasionally until softened. Spoon the vegetable mixture into a food processor or blender, then add half the broth and process until smooth.

4 Return to the pan and pour in the remaining broth. Bring the soup to a boil and adjust the seasoning before serving in bowls, garnished with a swirl of yogurt and a few curls of carrot.

MEDITERRANEAN TOMATO SOUP

Children will love this soup – especially if you use fancy shapes of pasta such as alphabet or animal shapes.

INGREDIENTS

Serves 4

1½ lb ripe plum tomatoes
1 medium onion, quartered
1 celery stalk
1 garlic clove
1 tbsp olive oil
1⅞ cups chicken broth
2 tbsp tomato paste
½ cup small pasta shapes
salt and black pepper
fresh cilantro or parsley, to garnish

1 Place the tomatoes, onion, celery, and garlic in a pan with the oil. Cover and cook over low heat for 40–45 minutes, shaking the pan occasionally, until very soft.

2 Spoon the vegetables into a food processor or blender and process until smooth. Press through a strainer, then return to the pan.

3 Stir in the broth and tomato paste and bring to a boil. Add the pasta and simmer gently for about 8 minutes, or until the pasta is tender. Add salt and pepper to taste, then sprinkle with cilantro or parsley and serve hot.

NUTRITION NOTES

Per portion:
Energy	112Kcals/474kJ
Fat	3.61g
Saturated fat	0.49g
Cholesterol	0
Fiber	2.68g

MUSHROOM, CELERY, AND GARLIC SOUP

INGREDIENTS

Serves 4

3 cups chopped mushrooms
4 celery stalks, chopped
3 garlic cloves
3 tbsp dry sherry or white wine
3⅔ cups chicken broth
2 tbsp Worcestershire sauce
1 tsp ground nutmeg
salt and black pepper
celery leaves, to garnish

NUTRITION NOTES

Per portion:
Energy	48Kcals/200kJ
Fat	1.09g
Saturated fat	0.11g
Cholesterol	0
Fiber	1.64g

1 Place the mushrooms, celery, and garlic in a pan and stir in the sherry or wine. Cover and cook over low heat for 30–40 minutes, until tender.

2 Add half the broth and purée in a food processor or blender until smooth. Return to the pan and add the remaining broth, the Worcestershire sauce, and nutmeg.

3 Bring to a boil, season, and serve hot, garnished with celery leaves.

BEET AND APRICOT SWIRL

This soup is most attractive if you swirl together the two colored mixtures, but if you prefer they can be mixed together to save on time and dishes.

INGREDIENTS

Serves 4

4 large cooked beets, coarsely chopped
1 small onion, coarsely chopped
2½ cups chicken broth
1 cup dried apricots
1 cup orange juice
salt and black pepper

1 Place the beets and half the onion in a pan with the broth. Bring to a boil, then reduce the heat, cover, and simmer for about 10 minutes. Purée in a food processor or blender.

2 Place the rest of the onion in a pan with the apricots and orange juice, cover, and simmer gently for about 15 minutes, until tender. Purée in a food processor or blender.

3 Return the two mixtures to the saucepans and reheat. Season to taste with salt and pepper, then swirl them together in individual soup bowls for a marbled effect.

COOK'S TIP
The apricot mixture should be the same consistency as the beet mixture – if it is too thick, then add a little more orange juice.

NUTRITION NOTES

Per portion:

Energy	135Kcals/569kJ
Fat	0.51g
Saturated fat	0.01g
Cholesterol	0
Fiber	4.43g

THAI-STYLE CORN SOUP

This is a very quick and easy soup, made in minutes. If you are using frozen shrimp, then defrost them first before adding to the soup.

INGREDIENTS

Serves 4

½ tsp sesame or sunflower oil
2 scallions, thinly sliced
1 garlic clove, crushed
2½ cups chicken broth
15oz can cream-style corn
1¼ cups cooked, peeled
   shrimp
1 tsp green chili paste or chili sauce
   (optional)
salt and black pepper
fresh cilantro leaves, to garnish

1 Heat the oil in a large heavy-based saucepan and sauté the scallions and garlic over medium heat for 1 minute, until softened, but not browned.

2 Stir in the chicken broth, cream-style corn, shrimp, and chili paste or sauce, if using.

3 Bring the soup to a boil, stirring occasionally. Season to taste, then serve at once, sprinkled with fresh cilantro leaves to garnish.

COOK'S TIP
If cream-style corn is not available, use ordinary canned corn, puréed in a food processor for a few seconds, until creamy yet with some texture left.

NUTRITION NOTES

Per portion:	
Energy	202Kcals/848kJ
Fat	3.01g
Saturated fat	0.43g
Cholesterol	45.56mg
Fiber	1.6g

MUSHROOM CROUSTADES

The rich mushroom flavor of this filling is heightened by the addition of Worcestershire sauce.

INGREDIENTS

Serves 2–4

1 short baguette, about 25cm/10in
2 tsp olive oil
9oz open cup mushrooms,
  quartered
2 tsp Worcestershire sauce
2 tsp lemon juice
2 tbsp skim milk
2 tbsp snipped fresh chives
salt and black pepper
snipped fresh chives, to garnish

1 Preheat the oven to 400°F. Cut the baguette in half lengthwise. Cut a scoop out of the soft middle of each using a sharp knife, leaving a thick border all the way around.

2 Brush the bread with oil, place on a baking sheet, and bake for about 6–8 minutes, until golden and crisp.

3 Place the mushrooms in a small saucepan with the Worcestershire sauce, lemon juice, and milk. Simmer for about 5 minutes, or until most of the liquid is evaporated.

4 Remove from the heat, then add the chives and seasoning. Spoon into the bread croustades and serve hot, garnished with snipped chives.

NUTRITION NOTES	
Per portion:	
Energy	324Kcals/1361kJ
Fat	6.4g
Saturated fat	1.27g
Cholesterol	0.3mg
Fiber	3.07g

TOMATO-PESTO TOASTIES

Ready-made pesto is high in fat but, as its flavor is so powerful, it can be used in very small amounts with good effect, as in these tasty toasties.

INGREDIENTS

Serves 2

2 *thick slices crusty bread*
3 *tbsp low fat cream cheese or low fat fromage frais*
2 *tsp red or green pesto*
1 *beefsteak tomato*
1 *red onion*
salt and black pepper

1 Place the bread slices under a hot broiler until golden brown on both sides, turning once. Leave to cool.

2 Mix together the low fat cream cheese and pesto in a small bowl until well blended, then spread thickly on the toasted bread.

3 Cut the beefsteak tomato and red onion, crosswise, into thin slices using a large sharp knife.

4 Arrange the slices, overlapping, on top of the toast and season with salt and pepper. Transfer the toasties to a broiler pan and broil until heated through, then serve immediately.

COOK'S TIP
Almost any type of crusty bread can be used for this recipe, but Italian olive oil bread and French bread will give the best flavor.

NUTRITION NOTES

Per portion:

Energy	177Kcals/741kJ
Fat	2.41g
Saturated fat	0.19g
Cholesterol	0.23mg
Fiber	2.2g

CHEESE AND SPINACH PUFFS

INGREDIENTS

Serves 6

1 cup cooked, chopped spinach
¾ cup cottage cheese
1 tsp ground nutmeg
2 egg whites
2 tbsp grated Parmesan cheese
salt and black pepper

1 Preheat the oven to 425°F. Brush six ramekin dishes with oil.

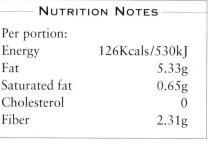

2 Mix together the spinach and cottage cheese in a small bowl, then add the nutmeg and seasoning to taste.

3 Whisk the egg whites in a separate bowl until stiff enough to hold soft peaks. Fold them evenly into the spinach mixture using a spatula or large metal spoon, then spoon the mixture into the oiled ramekins, dividing it evenly, and smooth the tops.

4 Sprinkle with the Parmesan and place on a baking sheet. Bake for 15–20 minutes, or until puffed and golden brown. Serve immediately.

NUTRITION NOTES

Per portion:

Energy	47Kcals/195kJ
Fat	1.32g
Saturated fat	0.52g
Cholesterol	2.79mg
Fiber	0.53g

LEMONY STUFFED ZUCCHINI

INGREDIENTS

Serves 4

4 zucchini, about 6oz each
1 tsp sunflower oil
1 garlic clove, crushed
1 tsp ground lemongrass
finely grated rind and juice of ½ lemon
scant ¼ cup cooked long-grain rice
6oz cherry tomatoes, halved
2 tbsp toasted cashews
salt and black pepper
sprigs of thyme, to garnish

NUTRITION NOTES

Per portion:

Energy	126Kcals/530kJ
Fat	5.33g
Saturated fat	0.65g
Cholesterol	0
Fiber	2.31g

1 Preheat the oven to 400°F. Halve the zucchini lengthwise and use a teaspoon to scoop out the centers. Blanch the shells in boiling water for 1 minute, then drain well.

2 Chop the zucchini flesh finely and place in a saucepan with the oil and garlic. Stir over moderate heat until softened, but not browned.

3 Stir in the lemongrass, lemon rind and juice, rice, tomatoes, and cashews. Season well and spoon into the zucchini shells. Place the shells in a baking pan and cover with foil.

4 Bake for 25–30 minutes or until the zucchini is tender, then serve hot, garnished with thyme sprigs.

CHICKEN PITAS WITH RED COLESLAW

Pitas are convenient for simple snacks and lunch boxes and it's easy to load in lots of fresh healthy ingredients.

INGREDIENTS

Serves 4
¼ red cabbage, finely shredded
1 small red onion, finely sliced
2 radishes, thinly sliced
1 red apple, peeled, cored, and grated
1 tbsp lemon juice
3 tbsp low fat fromage frais
1 cooked chicken breast without skin, about 6oz
4 large pitas or 8 small pitas
salt and black pepper
chopped fresh parsley, to garnish

1 Remove the tough central spine from the cabbage leaves, then finely shred the leaves using a large sharp knife. Place the shredded cabbage in a bowl and stir in the onion, radishes, apple, and lemon juice.

2 Stir the fromage frais into the shredded cabbage mixture and season well with salt and pepper. Thinly slice the cooked chicken breast and stir into the shredded cabbage mixture until well coated in fromage frais.

3 Toast the pitas until warmed, then split them along one edge using a round-bladed knife. Spoon the filling into the pitas, then garnish with chopped fresh parsley.

COOK'S TIP
If the filled pitas need to be made more than an hour in advance, line the pita breads with crisp lettuce leaves before adding the filling.

NUTRITION NOTES

Per portion:
Energy	232Kcals/976kJ
Fat	2.61g
Saturated fat	0.76g
Cholesterol	24.61mg
Fiber	2.97g

WHOLE-WHEAT SLTs

A quick, tasty snack or easy packed lunch with a healthy combination – sardines, lettuce, and tomatoes!

INGREDIENTS

Serves 2

2 small whole-wheat rolls
4¼ oz can sardines in olive oil
4 crisp green lettuce leaves, such as Bibb
1 beefsteak tomato, sliced
juice of ½ lemon
salt and black pepper

1 Slice the rolls in half crosswise using a sharp knife. Drain off the oil from the sardines into a small bowl, then brush the cut surfaces of the rolls with a small amount of the oil.

2 Cut or break the sardines into small pieces, then fill each roll with a lettuce leaf, some sliced tomato, and pieces of sardine, sprinkling the filling with a little lemon juice, and salt and pepper to taste.

3 Sandwich the rolls back together and press the lids down lightly with your hand. Serve at once.

NUTRITION NOTES

Per portion:

Energy	248Kcals/1042kJ
Fat	8.51g
Saturated fat	1.86g
Cholesterol	32.5mg
Fiber	3.01g

COOK'S TIP
As an alternative, replace the sardines with tuna packed in oil, or try mackerel fillets in oil and be generous with the black pepper.

TUNA CHILI TACOS

Tacos are a useful, quick snack – but you will need to use both hands to eat them!

INGREDIENTS

Makes 8

8 taco shells
14oz can red kidney beans, drained
½ cup low fat fromage frais
½ tsp chili sauce
2 scallions, chopped
1 tsp chopped fresh mint
½ small crisp lettuce, shredded
15oz can tuna chunks in water, drained
¾ cup shredded reduced-fat Cheddar cheese
8 cherry tomatoes, quartered
mint sprigs, to garnish

1 Warm the taco shells in a hot oven for a few minutes until crisp.

2 Mash the beans lightly with a fork, then stir in the fromage frais with the chili sauce, scallions, and mint.

3 Fill the taco shells with the shredded lettuce, the bean mixture, and tuna. Top the filled shells with the cheese and serve at once with the tomatoes, garnished with sprigs of mint.

NUTRITION NOTES

Per portion:

Energy	147Kcals/615kJ
Fat	2.42g
Saturated fat	1.13g
Cholesterol	29.69mg
Fiber	2.41g

POTATO SKINS WITH CAJUN DIP

No need to deep-fry potato skins for this treat – broiling crisps them up in no time.

INGREDIENTS

Serves 2

2 large baking potatoes
½ cup plain yogurt
1 garlic clove, crushed
1 tsp tomato paste
½ tsp green chili paste (or ½ small green chili, chopped
¼ tsp celery salt
salt and black pepper

1 Bake or microwave the potatoes until tender. Cut them in half and scoop out the flesh, leaving a thin layer on the skins. Keep the scooped out potato for another meal.

2 Cut each potato in half again then place the pieces skin-side down on a large baking sheet.

3 Broil for 4–5 minutes, or until crisp. Mix together the dip ingredients and serve with the potato skins.

NUTRITION NOTES

Per portion:

Energy	202Kcals/847kJ
Fat	0.93g
Saturated fat	0.34g
Cholesterol	2.3mg
Fiber	3.03g

CHINESE GARLIC MUSHROOMS

Tofu is high in protein and very low in fat, so it is a very useful food to keep handy for quick meals and snacks like this one.

INGREDIENTS

Serves 4

8 large open cup mushrooms
3 scallions, sliced
1 garlic clove, crushed
2 tbsp oyster sauce
10oz packet marinated tofu, cut into small dice
7oz can corn, drained
2 tsp sesame oil
salt and black pepper

1 Preheat the oven to 400°F. Finely chop the mushroom stalks and mix with the scallions, garlic, and oyster sauce.

2 Stir in the diced marinated tofu and corn, season well with salt and pepper, then carefully spoon the filling into the mushrooms.

3 Brush the edges of the mushrooms with the sesame oil. Arrange the stuffed mushrooms in a baking dish and bake for 12–15 minutes, until the mushrooms are just tender, then serve at once.

COOK'S TIP
If you prefer, omit the oyster sauce and use light soy sauce instead.

NUTRITION NOTES

Per portion:

Energy	137Kcals/575kJ
Fat	5.6g
Saturated fat	0.85g
Cholesterol	0
Fiber	1.96g

SURPRISE SCOTCH 'EGGS'

This reduced fat version of Scotch eggs is great for lunch boxes or picnics. If half-fat sausage meat isn't available, buy half-fat sausages or turkey sausages and remove the skins.

INGREDIENTS

Makes 3

*5 tbsp chopped parsley and snipped
    chives, mixed*
*½ cup low fat cream
    cheese*
1 lb half fat sausage meat
½ cup oatmeal
salt and black pepper
lettuce and tomato salad, to serve

1 Preheat the oven to 400°F. Mix together the herbs, cheese, and seasonings, then roll into three even-sized balls.

2 Divide the sausage meat into thirds and press each piece out to a round, about ½ in thick.

3 Wrap each cheese ball in a piece of sausage meat, smoothing all over to enclose the cheese completely. Spread out the oatmeal on a plate and roll the balls in the oatmeal, using your hands to coat them evenly.

4 Place the balls on a baking sheet and bake for 30–35 minutes or until golden. Serve hot or cold, with a lettuce and tomato salad.

NUTRITION NOTES	
Per portion:	
Energy	352Kcals/1476kJ
Fat	15.94g
Saturated fat	0.29g
Cholesterol	66.38mg
Fiber	3.82g

SALMON PARCELS

Serve these little savory parcels just as they are for a snack, or with a pool of fresh tomato sauce for a special appetizer.

INGREDIENTS

Makes 12

3½oz can red or pink salmon
1 tbsp chopped fresh cilantro
4 scallions, finely chopped
4 sheets fila pastry
sunflower oil, for brushing
scallions and lettuce, to serve

COOK'S TIP
When you are using fila pastry, it is important to prevent it drying out; cover any you are not using with a dish towel or plastic wrap.

---

1 Preheat the oven to 400°F. Lightly oil a baking sheet. Drain the salmon, discarding any skin and bones, then place in a bowl.

2 Flake the salmon with a fork and mix with the fresh cilantro and scallions.

3 Place a single sheet of fila pastry on a work surface and brush lightly with oil. Place another sheet on top. Cut into six squares, each about 4in. Repeat with the remaining pastry, to make 12 squares.

4 Place a spoonful of the salmon mixture on each square. Brush the edges of the pastry with oil, then draw together, pressing to seal. Place on a baking sheet and bake for 12–15 minutes, until golden. Serve warm, with scallions and lettuce.

NUTRITION NOTES	
Per portion:	
Energy	25Kcals/107kJ
Fat	1.16g
Saturated fat	0.23g
Cholesterol	2.55mg
Fiber	0.05g

TOMATO-CHEESE TARTS

These crisp little tartlets are easier to make than they look. Best eaten fresh from the oven.

INGREDIENTS

Serves 4

2 sheets fila pastry
1 egg white
½ cup low fat cream cheese
handful fresh basil leaves
3 small tomatoes, sliced
salt and black pepper

1 Preheat the oven to 400°F. Brush the sheets of fila pastry lightly with egg white and cut into sixteen 4 in squares.

2 Layer the squares in twos, in eight muffin tins. Spoon the cheese into the pastry cases. Season with black pepper and top with basil leaves.

3 Arrange tomatoes on the tarts, add seasoning, and bake for 10-12 minutes, until golden. Serve warm.

NUTRITION NOTES	
Per portion:	
Energy	50Kcals/210kJ
Fat	0.33g
Saturated fat	0.05g
Cholesterol	0.29mg
Fiber	0.25g

EGGPLANT SUNFLOWER PÂTÉ

Serves 4
1 large eggplant
1 garlic clove, crushed
1 tbsp lemon juice
2 tbsp sunflower seeds
3 tbsp plain low fat yogurt
handful fresh cilantro or parsley
black pepper
black olives, to garnish

1 Cut the eggplant in half and place, cut-side down, on a baking sheet. Place under a hot broiler for 15–20 minutes, until the skin is blackened and the flesh is soft. Leave for a few minutes, to cool slightly.

2 Scoop the flesh of the eggplant into a food processor. Add the garlic, lemon juice, sunflower seeds, and yogurt. Process until smooth.

3 Coarsely chop the fresh cilantro or parsley and mix in. Season, then spoon into a serving dish. Top with olives and serve with vegetable sticks.

NUTRITION NOTES

Per portion:	
Energy	71Kcals/298kJ
Fat	4.51g
Saturated fat	0.48g
Cholesterol	0.45mg
Fiber	2.62g

BELL PEPPER DIPS WITH CRUDITÉS

Make one or both of these colorful vegetable dips – if you have time to make both they look spectacular together.

Serves 4–6
2 medium red bell peppers, halved and seeded
2 medium yellow bell peppers, halved and seeded
2 garlic cloves
2 tbsp lemon juice
4 tsp olive oil
½ cup fresh white bread crumbs
salt and black pepper
fresh vegetables, for dipping

1 Place the bell peppers in separate saucepans with a peeled clove of garlic. Add just enough water to cover.

2 Bring to a boil, then cover and simmer for 15 minutes until tender. Drain, cool, then purée separately in a food processor or blender, adding half the lemon juice and olive oil to each.

3 Stir half the bread crumbs into each and season to taste with salt and pepper. Serve the dips with a selection of fresh vegetables for dipping.

NUTRITION NOTES

Per portion:	
Energy	103Kcals/432kJ
Fat	3.7g
Saturated fat	0.47g
Cholesterol	0
Fiber	2.77g

MEAT DISHES

There's no reason why meat should not be a valuable part of a low fat, low cholesterol diet, but you need to make careful choices when shopping, and adapt preparation and cooking methods to keep fats to a minimum. Remember that even lean meat has hidden fat, so broiling or roasting on a rack is an advantage, and any added fats should be low in saturates and used in moderation. A fat-trimmed roast needn't be dry, especially if you seal it with a moist, savory crust as in Pork Roast in a Blanket. Even for casseroles, there's often no need to seal the meat in fat first – a nonstick pan will seal the meat in its own fat. Or choose stir-frying, which quickly seals the meat with just a touch of oil.

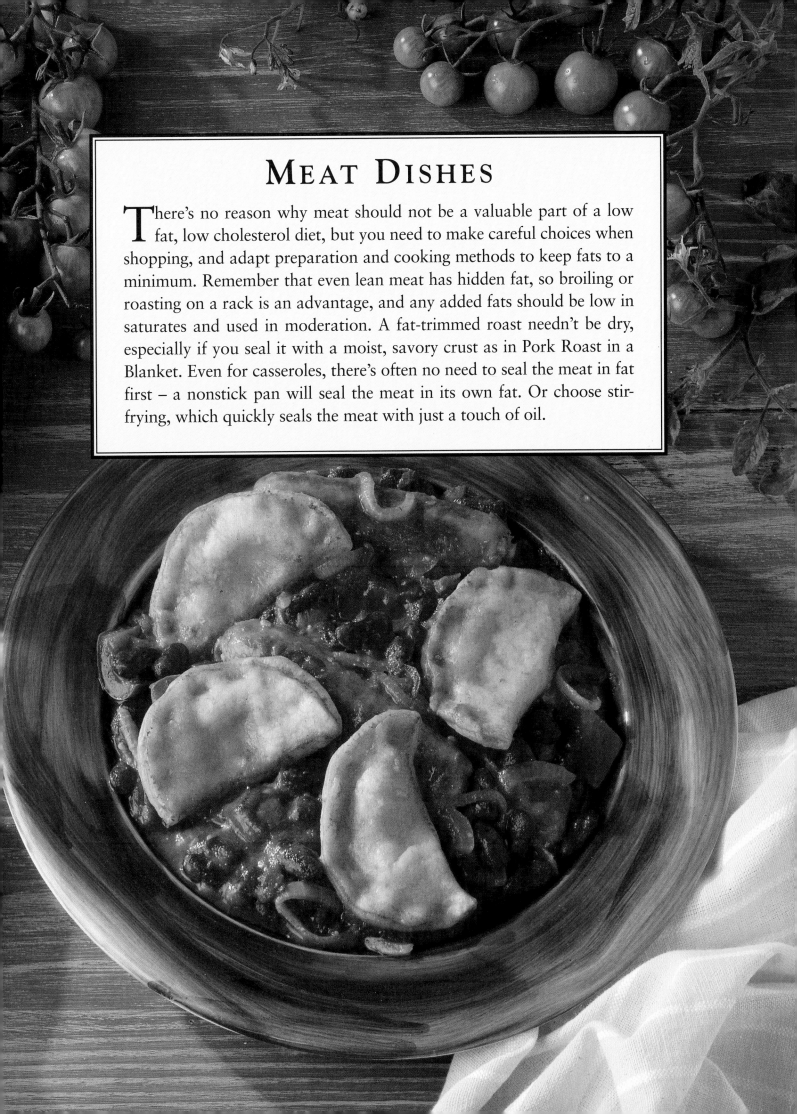

PORK AND CELERY POPOVERS

Lower in fat than they look, and a good way to make the meat go further, these little popovers will be popular with children.

INGREDIENTS

Serves 4
sunflower oil, for brushing
1¼ cup flour
1 egg white
1 cup skim milk
½ cup water
12 oz lean ground pork
2 celery stalks, finely chopped
3 tbsp oatmeal
2 tbsp snipped chives
1 tbsp Worcestershire sauce
salt and black pepper

1 Preheat the oven to 425°F. Brush 12 deep muffin pans with a small amount of oil.

2 Place the flour in a bowl and make a well in the center. Add the egg white and milk and gradually beat in the flour. Gradually add the water, beating until smooth and bubbly.

3 Place the ground pork, celery, oatmeal, chives, Worcestershire sauce, and seasoning in a bowl and mix well. Mold the mixture into 12 small balls and place in the muffin pans.

4 Cook for 10 minutes, remove from the oven, and quickly pour the batter into the pans. Cook for 20–25 minutes more, or until puffed and golden brown. Serve hot with thin gravy and fresh vegetables.

NUTRITION NOTES	
Per portion:	
Energy	344Kcals/1443kJ
Fat	9.09g
Saturated fat	2.7g
Cholesterol	61.62mg
Fiber	2.37g

BEEF AND MUSHROOM BURGERS

It's worth making your own burgers to cut down on fat – in these the meat is extended with mushrooms for extra fiber.

INGREDIENTS

Serves 4

1 small onion, *chopped*
2 cups small cup mushrooms
1 lb lean ground beef
1 cup fresh whole-wheat bread crumbs
1 tsp dried mixed herbs
1 tbsp tomato paste
flour, for shaping
salt and black pepper

1 Place the onion and mushrooms in a food processor and process until finely chopped. Add the beef, bread crumbs, herbs, tomato paste and seasonings. Process for a few seconds, until the mixture binds together but still has some texture.

2 Divide the mixture into 8–10 pieces, then press into burger shapes using lightly floured hands.

3 Cook the burgers in a nonstick skillet, or under a hot broiler for 12-15 minutes, turning once, until evenly cooked. Serve with relish and lettuce, in burger buns or pita bread.

COOK'S TIP
The mixture is soft, so handle carefully and use a metal spatula for turning to prevent the burgers from breaking during cooking.

NUTRITION NOTES

Per portion:

Energy	196Kcals/822kJ
Fat	5.9g
Saturated fat	2.21g
Cholesterol	66.37mg
Fiber	1.6g

CURRIED LAMB AND LENTILS

This colorful curry is packed with protein and low in fat.

INGREDIENTS

Serves 4

8 lean, boneless lamb leg steaks, about
    1¼ lb total weight
1 medium onion, chopped
2 medium carrots, diced
1 celery stalk, chopped
1 tbsp hot curry paste
2 tbsp tomato paste
2 cups broth
1 cup green lentils
salt and black pepper
fresh cilantro leaves, to garnish
boiled rice, to serve

1 In a large, nonstick pan, cook the lamb steaks without fat until browned, turning once.

2 Add the vegetables and cook for 2 minutes, then stir in the curry paste, tomato paste, broth, and lentils.

3 Bring to a boil, cover, and simmer gently for 30 minutes until tender. Add more broth, if necessary. Season and serve with cilantro and rice.

NUTRITION NOTES

Per portion:

Energy	375Kcals/1575kJ
Fat	13.03g
Saturated fat	5.34g
Cholesterol	98.75mg
Fiber	6.11g

GOLDEN PORK AND APRICOT CASSEROLE

The rich golden color and warm spicy flavor of this simple casserole make it ideal for chilly winter days.

INGREDIENTS

Serves 4

4 lean pork loin chops
1 medium onion, thinly sliced
2 yellow bell peppers, seeded and
    sliced
2 tsp medium hot curry powder
1 tbsp flour
1 cup chicken broth
⅔ cup dried apricots
2 tbsp whole-grain mustard
salt and black pepper

1 Trim the excess fat from the pork and cook without fat in a large, heavy or nonstick pan until lightly browned.

2 Add the onion and bell peppers to the pan and stir over moderate heat for 5 minutes. Stir in the curry powder and the flour.

3 Add the broth, stirring, then add the apricots and mustard. Cover and simmer for 25–30 minutes, until tender. Adjust the seasoning and serve hot, with rice or new potatoes.

NUTRITION NOTES

Per portion:

Energy	289Kcals/1213kJ
Fat	10.03g
Saturated fat	3.23g
Cholesterol	82.8mg
Fiber	4.86g

COUNTRY PORK WITH PARSLEY COBBLER

This hearty casserole is a
complete main course in one pot.

INGREDIENTS

Serves 4
1 lb boneless pork shoulder, diced
1 small rutabaga, diced
2 carrots, sliced
2 parsnips, sliced
2 leeks, sliced
2 celery stalks, sliced
3⅔ cups boiling beef broth
2 tbsp tomato paste
2 tbsp chopped fresh parsley
¼ cup pearl barley
celery salt and black pepper

For the topping
1 cup flour
1 tsp baking powder
6 tbsp low fat fromage frais
3 tbsp chopped fresh parsley

1 Preheat the oven to 350°. Cook the pork without fat, in a nonstick pan until lightly browned.

2 Add the vegetables to the pan and stir over medium heat until lightly colored. Tip into a large casserole dish, then stir in the broth, tomato paste, parsley, and pearl barley.

3 Season with celery salt and pepper, then cover and place in the oven for about 1–1¼ hours, until the pork and vegetables are tender.

4 For the topping, sift the flour and baking powder with seasoning, then stir in the fromage frais and parsley with enough cold water to mix to a soft dough. Roll out to about ½ inch thickness and cut into 12–16 triangles.

5 Remove the casserole from the oven and raise the temperature to 425°F.

6 Arrange the triangles over the casserole, overlapping. Bake for 15–20 minutes, until puffed and golden.

NUTRITION NOTES

Per portion:
Energy	461Kcals/1936kJ
Fat	10.55g
Saturated fat	3.02g
Cholesterol	77.85mg
Fiber	9.44g

BEEF STRIPS WITH ORANGE AND GINGER

Stir-frying is one of the best ways to cook with the minimum of fat. It's also one of the quickest ways to cook, but you do need to choose tender meat.

INGREDIENTS

Serves 4

1 lb lean beef rump, fillet, or sirloin, cut into thin strips
finely grated rind and juice of 1 orange
1 tbsp light soy sauce
1 tsp cornstarch
1in piece ginger root, finely chopped
2 tsp sesame oil
1 large carrot, cut into thin strips
2 scallions, thinly sliced

1 Place the beef strips in a bowl and sprinkle over the orange rind and juice. If possible, leave to marinate for at least 30 minutes.

2 Drain the liquid from the meat and set aside, then mix the meat with the soy sauce, cornstarch, and ginger.

3 Heat the oil in a wok or large frying pan and add the beef. Stir-fry for 1 minute until lightly colored, then add the carrot and stir-fry for 2–3 minutes more.

4 Stir in the scallions and reserved liquid, then cook, stirring, until boiling and thickened. Serve hot with rice noodles or plain boiled rice.

NUTRITION NOTES

Per portion:

Energy	175Kcals/730kJ
Fat	6.81g
Saturated fat	2.31g
Cholesterol	66.37mg
Fiber	0.67g

PAN-FRIED MEDITERRANEAN LAMB

The warm summery flavors of the Mediterranean are combined for a simple weekday meal.

INGREDIENTS

Serves 4

8 lean lamb rib chops
1 medium onion, thinly sliced
2 red bell peppers, seeded and sliced
14oz can plum tomatoes
1 garlic clove, crushed
3 tbsp chopped fresh basil leaves
2 tbsp chopped black olives
salt and black pepper

1 Trim any excess fat from the lamb, then cook without fat in a nonstick pan until golden brown.

2 Add the onion and bell peppers to the pan. Cook, stirring, for a few minutes to soften, then add the plum tomatoes, garlic, and basil.

3 Cover and simmer for 20 minutes or until the lamb is tender. Stir in the olives, season, and serve hot with pasta.

NUTRITION NOTES

Per portion:

Energy	224Kcals/939kJ
Fat	10.17g
Saturated fat	4.32g
Cholesterol	79mg
Fiber	2.48g

BACON KOFTAS

These easy koftas are good for outdoor summer barbecues, served with lots of salad.

INGREDIENTS

Serves 4

8oz lean bacon, coarsely chopped
1 cup fresh whole-wheat bread crumbs
2 scallions, chopped
15ml/1 tbsp chopped fresh parsley
finely grated rind of 1 lemon
1 egg white
black pepper
paprika
lemon rind and fresh parsley leaves, to garnish

1 Place the bacon in a food processor together with the bread crumbs, scallions, parsley, lemon rind, egg white, and pepper. Process the mixture until it is finely chopped and begins to bind together.

2 Divide the bacon mixture into eight, even-sized pieces and shape into long ovals around eight wooden or bamboo skewers.

3 Sprinkle the koftas with paprika and cook under a hot broiler or on a barbecue for about 8–10 minutes, turning occasionally, until browned and cooked through. Garnish with lemon rind and parsley leaves, then serve hot with lemon rice and salad.

NUTRITION NOTES

Per portion:

Energy	128Kcals/538kJ
Fat	4.7g
Saturated fat	1.61g
Cholesterol	10.13mg
Fiber	1.33g

LAMB PIE WITH POTATO CRUST

A pleasant change from meat and potatoes – healthier, too.

INGREDIENTS

Serves 4

1½ lb potatoes, diced
2 tbsp skim milk
1 tbsp whole-grain or French mustard
1 lb lean ground lamb
1 onion, chopped
2 celery stalks, sliced
2 carrots, diced
⅔ cup beef broth
4 tbsp oatmeal
1 tbsp Worcestershire sauce
2 tbsp fresh chopped rosemary, or
    2 tsp dried
salt and black pepper

1 Cook the potatoes in boiling, lightly salted water until tender. Drain and mash until smooth, then stir in the milk and mustard. Meanwhile, preheat the oven to 400°F.

2 Break up the lamb with a fork and cook without fat in a nonstick pan until lightly browned. Add the onion, celery, and carrots to the pan and cook for 2–3 minutes, stirring.

3 Stir in the broth and oatmeal. Bring to a boil, then add the Worcestershire sauce and rosemary, and season to taste with salt and pepper.

4 Turn the meat mixture into a 1.8 litre/3 pint/7 cup ovenproof dish and spread over the potato topping evenly, swirling with the edge of a knife. Bake for 30–35 minutes, or until golden. Serve hot with fresh vegetables.

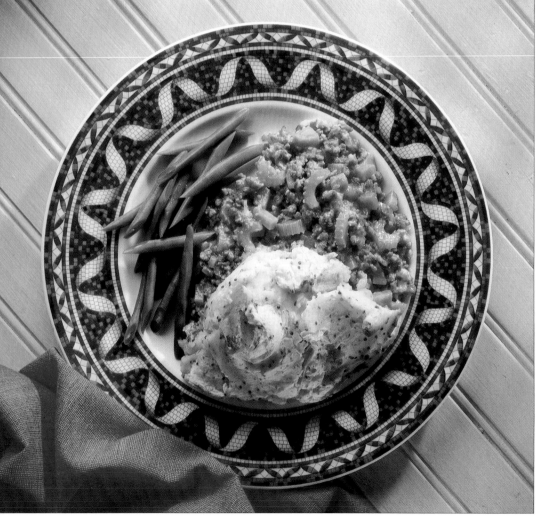

NUTRITION NOTES

Per portion:

Energy	422Kcals/1770kJ
Fat	12.41g
Saturated fat	5.04g
Cholesterol	89.03mg
Fiber	5.07g

SAUSAGE AND BEANS WITH DUMPLINGS

Sausages needn't be totally banned on a low fat diet, but choose them carefully. If you are unable to find a reduced-fat variety, choose turkey sausages instead, and always drain off any fat during cooking.

INGREDIENTS

Serves 4
1 lb half-fat sausages
1 medium onion, thinly sliced
1 green bell pepper, seeded and diced
1 small red chili, sliced, or ½ tsp chili
  sauce
14oz can chopped tomatoes
1 cup beef broth
15oz can red kidney beans, drained
salt and black pepper

For the dumplings
2½ cups flour
2 tsp baking powder
1 cup cottage cheese

1 Cook the sausages without fat in a nonstick pan until brown. Add the onion and pepper. Stir in the chili, tomatoes, and broth; bring to a boil.

NUTRITION NOTES

Per portion:

Energy	574Kcals/2409kJ
Fat	13.09g
Saturated fat	0.15g
Cholesterol	52.31mg
Fiber	9.59g

2 Cover and simmer gently for 15–20 minutes, then add the beans and bring to a boil.

3 To make the dumplings, sift the flour and baking powder together and add enough water to mix to a firm dough. Roll out thinly and stamp out 16–18 rounds using a 3in cutter.

4 Place a small spoonful of cottage cheese on each round and bring the edges of the dough together, pinching to enclose. Arrange the dumplings over the sausages in the pan, cover the pan, and simmer for 10–12 minutes, until the dumplings are puffed. Serve hot.

GREEK LAMB PIE

INGREDIENTS

Serves 4

sunflower oil, for brushing
1 lb lean ground lamb
1 medium onion, sliced
1 garlic clove, crushed
14oz can plum tomatoes
2 tbsp chopped fresh mint
1 tsp ground nutmeg
12oz young spinach leaves
10 oz packet fila pastry
1 tsp sesame seeds
salt and black pepper

1 Preheat the oven to 400°F. Lightly oil a 8½ in round spring form pan.

2 Cook the lamb and onion without fat in a nonstick pan until golden. Add the garlic, tomatoes, mint, nutmeg, and seasoning. Bring to a boil, stirring. Simmer, stirring occasionally, until most of the liquid has evaporated.

3 Wash the spinach and remove any tough stalks, then cook in only the water clinging to the leaves for about 2 minutes, until wilted.

4 Lightly brush each sheet of fila pastry with oil and lay in overlapping layers in the pan, leaving enough overhanging to wrap over the top.

5 Spoon in the meat and spinach, then wrap the pastry over to enclose, scrunching it slightly. Sprinkle with sesame seeds and bake for about 25–30 minutes, or until golden and crisp. Serve hot, with salad or vegetables.

NUTRITION NOTES

Per portion:

Energy	444Kcals/1865kJ
Fat	15.36g
Saturated fat	5.51g
Cholesterol	88.87mg
Fiber	3g

PORK ROAST IN A BLANKET

INGREDIENTS

Serves 4

3 lb lean pork loin joint
1 eating apple, cored and grated
¾ cup fresh bread crumbs
2 tbsp chopped hazelnuts
1 tbsp Dijon mustard
1 tbsp snipped fresh chives
salt and black pepper

1 If necessary, trim the roast, leaving only a thin layer of fat.

2 Preheat the oven to 425°F. Place the meat on a rack in a roasting pan, cover the meat with foil, and roast for 1 hour, then reduce the oven temperature to 350°F.

3 Mix together the apple, bread crumbs, nuts, mustard, chives, and seasoning. Remove the foil and spread the bread crumb mixture over the fat surface of the meat.

4 Roast the pork for 45–60 minutes, or until the juices run clear. Serve in slices with gravy.

NUTRITION NOTES

Per portion:

Energy	367Kcals/1540kJ
Fat	18.73g
Saturated fat	5.19g
Cholesterol	129.38mg
Fiber	1.5g

RUBY PORK CHOPS

This sweet, tangy sauce works well with lean pork chops.

INGREDIENTS

Serves 4
1 ruby grapefruit
4 lean boneless pork chops
3 tbsp red currant jelly
black pepper

NUTRITION NOTES

Per portion:	
Energy	215Kcals/904kJ
Fat	8.40g
Saturated fat	3.02g
Cholesterol	20.25mg
Fiber	0.81g

1 Cut away all the peel and pith from the grapefruit, using a sharp knife, and carefully remove the segments, catching the juice in a bowl.

2 Cook the pork chops in a nonstick skillet without fat, turning them once, until golden and cooked.

3 Add the reserved grapefruit juice and red currant jelly to the pan and stir until melted. Add the grapefruit segments, then season with pepper, and serve hot with fresh vegetables.

JAMAICAN BEAN STEW

If pumpkin is not available, use any other type of squash, or try rutabaga instead. This recipe is a good one to double – or even triple – for a crowd.

INGREDIENTS

Serves 4
1 lb stewing beef, diced
1 small pumpkin, about 1 lb, flesh diced
1 medium onion, chopped
1 green bell pepper, seeded and sliced
1 tbsp paprika
2 garlic cloves, crushed
1 in piece fresh ginger root, chopped
14oz can chopped tomatoes
1 cup baby corn
1 cup beef broth
15oz can chick-peas, drained
15oz can red kidney beans, drained
salt and black pepper

1 Cook the diced beef without fat in a large flameproof casserole, stirring to seal it on all sides.

2 Stir in the pumpkin, onion, and pepper, cook for 2 minutes more, then add the paprika, garlic, and ginger.

3 Stir in the tomatoes, corn, and broth, then bring to a boil. Cover and simmer for 40–45 minutes or until tender. Add the chick peas and beans, and heat thoroughly. Adjust the seasoning with salt and pepper to taste. Serve hot, with couscous or rice.

NUTRITION NOTES

Per portion:	
Energy	357Kcals/1500kJ
Fat	8.77g
Saturated fat	2.11g
Cholesterol	66.37mg
Fiber	10.63g

POULTRY AND GAME

Poultry and game are obvious choices for a low fat diet, as they are mostly very low in fat, and much of the fat they do contain is low in saturates. Chicken, always a favorite choice for family meals, is endlessly versatile and economical, and is well suited to low fat cooking methods. Turkey, also low fat, is now available in so many different cuts that it's almost interchangeable with chicken, and ground turkey can take the place of beef in healthy, savory bakes and pasta dishes. For a change, introduce game into family meals, as it is particularly low in saturated fat and just as simple to cook as chicken. Even high-fat poultry such as duck can be cooked in new ways to reduce fat – and add to the flavor.

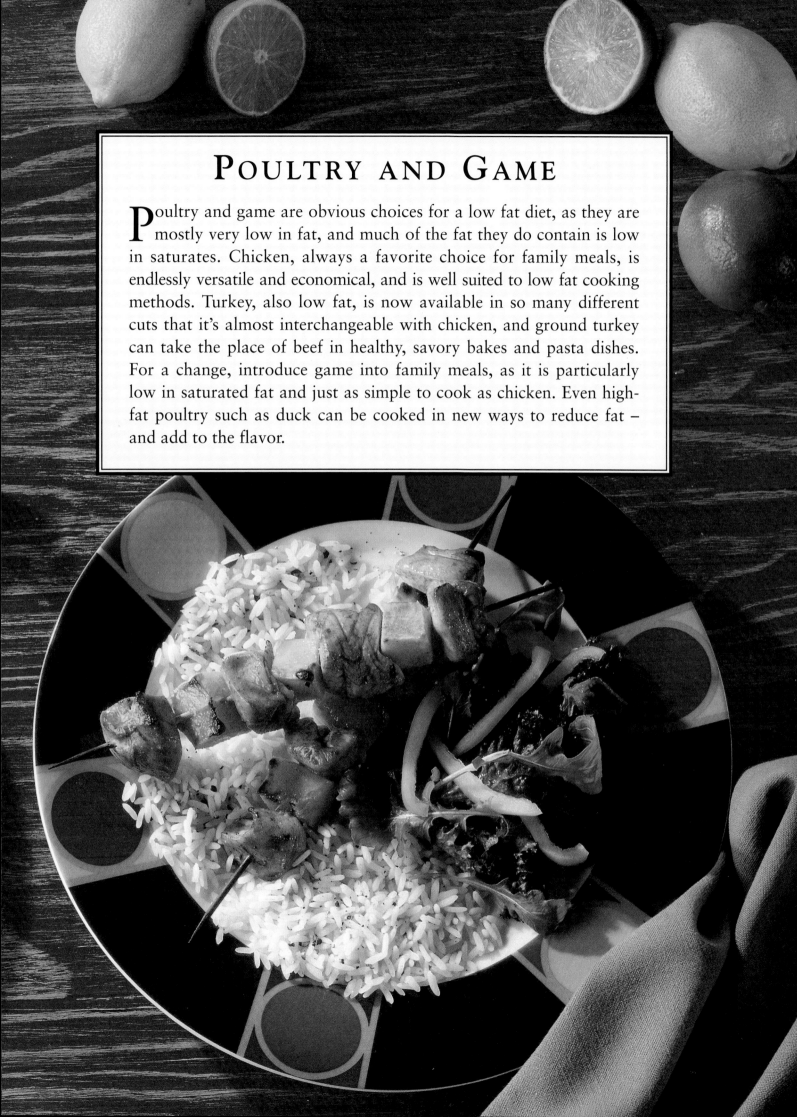

TURKEY PASTITSIO

A traditional Greek pastitsio is a rich, high-fat dish made with ground beef, but this lighter version is just as tasty.

Serves 4–6
1 lb lean ground turkey
1 large onion, finely chopped
4 tbsp tomato paste
1 cup red wine or broth
1 tsp ground cinnamon
2½ cups macaroni
1¼ cups skim milk
2 tbsp sunflower margarine
3 tbsp flour
1 tsp ground nutmeg
2 tomatoes, sliced
4 tbsp whole-wheat bread crumbs
salt and black pepper
green salad, to serve

1 Preheat the oven to 425°F. Cook the turkey and chopped onion in a nonstick pan without fat, stirring until lightly browned.

2 Stir in the tomato paste, red wine or broth, and cinnamon. Season, then cover and simmer for 5 minutes.

3 Cook the macaroni in boiling, salted water until just tender, then drain. Layer with the meat mixture in a wide ovenproof dish.

4 Place the milk, margarine, and flour in a saucepan and whisk over a moderate heat until thickened and smooth. Add the nutmeg, and salt and pepper to taste.

5 Pour the sauce evenly over the pasta and meat. Arrange the tomato slices on top and sprinkle lines of bread crumbs over the surface.

6 Bake for 30–35 minutes, or until golden brown and bubbling. Serve hot, with a green salad.

NUTRITION NOTES	
Per portion:	
Energy	566Kcals/2382kJ
Fat	8.97g
Saturated fat	1.76g
Cholesterol	57.06mg
Fiber	4.86g

TUSCAN CHICKEN

This simple peasant casserole has all the flavors of traditional Tuscan ingredients. The wine can be replaced by chicken broth.

INGREDIENTS

Serves 4

8 chicken thighs, skinned
1 tsp olive oil
1 medium onion, sliced thinly
2 red bell peppers, seeded and sliced
1 garlic clove, crushed
1¼ cups puréed tomatoes
⅔ cup dry white wine
large sprig fresh oregano, or 1 tsp dried
   oregano
14oz can cannelini beans, drained
3 tbsp fresh bread crumbs
salt and black pepper

1 Cook the chicken in the oil in a nonstick or heavy pan until golden brown. Remove and keep hot. Add the onion and bell peppers to the pan and gently sauté until softened, but not brown. Stir in the garlic.

2 Add the chicken, tomatoes, wine, and oregano. Season well, bring to a boil, then cover the pan tightly.

3 Lower the heat and simmer gently, stirring occasionally for 30–35 minutes or until the chicken is tender and the juices run clear, not pink, when pierced with the point of a knife.

4 Stir in the cannelini beans and simmer for 5 minutes more, until heated through. Sprinkle with the bread crumbs and cook under a broiler until golden brown.

NUTRITION NOTES

Per portion:

Energy	248Kcals/1045kJ
Fat	7.53g
Saturated fat	2.06g
Cholesterol	73mg
Fiber	4.03g

MOROCCAN ROCK CORNISH HENS

INGREDIENTS

Serves 4

1½ cups cooked long-grain rice
1 small onion, chopped finely
finely grated rind and juice of 1 lemon
2 tbsp chopped mint
3 tbsp chopped dried apricots
2 tbsp plain yogurt
2 tsp ground turmeric
2 tsp ground cumin
2 x 1lb Rock Cornish hens
salt and black pepper
lemon slices and mint sprigs, to garnish

1 Preheat the oven to 400°F. Mix together the rice, onion, lemon rind, mint, and apricots. Stir in half each of the lemon juice, yogurt, turmeric, cumin, and salt and pepper.

2 Stuff the hens with the rice mixture at the neck end only. Any spare stuffing can be served separately. Place the hens on a rack in a roasting pan.

3 Mix together the remaining lemon juice, yogurt, turmeric, and cumin, then brush this over the hens. Cover loosely with foil and roast in the oven for 30 minutes.

4 Remove the foil and roast for a further 15 minutes, or until golden brown and the juices run clear, not pink, when pierced.

5 Cut the hens in half with a sharp knife or poultry shears, and serve with the reserved rice. Garnish with lemon slices and fresh mint.

NUTRITION NOTES

Per portion:

Energy	219Kcals/919kJ
Fat	6.02g
Saturated fat	1.87g
Cholesterol	71.55mg
Fiber	1.12g

STICKY GINGER CHICKEN

INGREDIENTS

Serves 4

2 tbsp lemon juice
2 tbsp brown sugar
1 tsp grated fresh ginger root
2 tsp soy sauce
8 chicken drumsticks, skinned
black pepper

NUTRITION NOTES

Per portion:

Energy	162Kcals/679kJ
Fat	5.58g
Saturated fat	1.84g
Cholesterol	73mg
Fiber	0.08g

1 Mix together the lemon juice, sugar, ginger, soy sauce, and pepper.

2 With a sharp knife, slash the chicken drumsticks about three times through the thickest part, then toss the chicken in the glaze.

3 Cook the chicken under a broiler, or barbecue, turning occasionally and brushing with the glaze, until the chicken is golden and the juices run clear, not pink, when pierced. Serve on a bed of lettuce, with crusty bread.

TURKEY SPIRALS

These little spirals may look difficult, but they're very simple to make, and a very good way to pep up plain turkey.

INGREDIENTS

Serves 4

4 thinly sliced turkey breasts, about
  3½oz each
4 tsp tomato paste
½ cup large basil leaves
1 garlic clove, crushed
1 tbsp skim milk
2 tbsp whole-wheat flour
salt and black pepper
fresh tomato sauce and pasta with fresh
  basil, to serve

1 Place the turkey steaks on a board. If too thick, flatten them slightly by beating with a rolling pin.

2 Spread each turkey breast with tomato paste, then top with a few leaves of basil, a little crushed garlic, and salt and pepper.

3 Roll up firmly around the filling and secure with a toothpick. Brush with milk and sprinkle with flour to coat lightly.

4 Place the spirals on a foil-lined broiler pan. Cook under a broiler for 15–20 minutes, turning them occasionally, until thoroughly cooked. Serve hot, sliced with a spoonful or two of fresh tomato sauce and pasta, sprinkled with fresh basil.

COOK'S TIP
When flattening the turkey breasts with a rolling pin, place them between two sheets of plastic wrap.

NUTRITION NOTES

Per portion:

Energy	123Kcals/518kJ
Fat	1.21g
Saturated fat	0.36g
Cholesterol	44.17mg
Fiber	0.87g

CARIBBEAN CHICKEN KABOBS

These kabobs have a rich, sunshine Caribbean flavor and the marinade keeps them moist without the need for oil. Serve with a colorful salad and rice.

INGREDIENTS

Serves 4
1¼ lb boneless chicken breasts, skinned
finely grated rind of 1 lime
2 tbsp lime juice
1 tbsp rum or sherry
1 tbsp brown sugar
1 tsp ground cinnamon
2 mangoes, peeled and cubed
rice and salad, to serve

1 Cut the chicken into bite-sized chunks and place in a bowl with the lime rind and juice, rum, sugar, and cinnamon. Toss well, cover, and leave to marinate for 1 hour.

2 Save the juices and thread the chicken onto four wooden skewers, alternating with the mango cubes.

3 Cook the skewers under a broiler, or barbecue, for 8–10 minutes, turning occasionally and basting with the juices, until the chicken is tender and golden brown. Serve at once, with rice and salad.

COOK'S TIP
The rum or sherry adds a lovely rich flavor, but it is optional so can be omitted if you prefer to avoid the added alcohol.

NUTRITION NOTES

Per portion:

Energy	218Kcals/918kJ
Fat	4.17g
Saturated fat	1.33g
Cholesterol	53.75mg
Fiber	2.26g

CHILI-CHICKEN COUSCOUS

Couscous is a very easy alternative to rice and makes a good base for all kinds of ingredients.

INGREDIENTS

Serves 4

2 cups couscous
4 cups boiling water
1 tsp olive oil
14oz chicken without skin and bone, diced
1 yellow bell pepper, seeded and sliced
2 large zucchini, sliced thickly
1 small green chili, thinly sliced, or 1 tsp chili sauce
1 large tomato, diced
15oz can chick peas, drained
salt and black pepper
cilantro or parsley sprigs to garnish

1 Place couscous in a large bowl and pour over boiling water. Cover and let stand for 30 minutes.

2 Heat the oil in a large, nonstick pan and stir-fry the chicken quickly to seal, then reduce the heat.

3 Stir in the pepper, zucchini, and chili or sauce and cook for 10 minutes, until the vegetables are softened.

4 Stir in the tomato and chick peas, then add the couscous. Adjust the seasoning and stir over moderate heat until hot. Serve garnished with sprigs of fresh cilantro or parsley.

NUTRITION NOTES

Per portion:

Energy	363Kcals/1525kJ
Fat	8.09g
Saturated fat	1.68g
Cholesterol	57mg
Fiber	4.38g

TURKEY AND BEAN BAKE

INGREDIENTS

Serves 4

1 medium eggplant, thinly sliced
1 tbsp olive oil, for brushing
1 lb turkey breast, diced
1 medium onion, chopped
14oz can chopped tomatoes
15oz can red kidney beans, drained
1 tbsp paprika
1 tbsp fresh chopped thyme, or 1 tsp dried
1 tsp chili sauce
1½ cups plain yogurt
½ tsp ground nutmeg
salt and black pepper

1 Preheat the oven to 375°F. Arrange the eggplant in a colander and sprinkle with salt.

2 Leave the eggplant for 30 minutes, then rinse and pat dry. Brush a nonstick pan with oil and cook the eggplant in batches, turning once, until golden.

3 Remove the eggplant, add the turkey and onion to the pan, then cook until lightly browned. Stir in the tomatoes, beans, paprika, thyme, chili sauce, and salt and pepper. In a separate bowl, mix together the yogurt and ground nutmeg.

4 Layer the meat and eggplant in an ovenproof dish, finishing with eggplant. Spread over the yogurt and bake for 50–60 minutes, until golden.

NUTRITION NOTES

Per portion:

Energy	370Kcals/1555kJ
Fat	13.72g
Saturated fat	5.81g
Cholesterol	66.5mg
Fiber	7.38g

OATMEAL-COATED CHICKEN WITH SAGE

Oatmeal makes a good coating for savory foods, and offers a good way to add extra fiber.

INGREDIENTS

Serves 4

3 tbsp skim milk
2 tsp plain mustard
½ cup oatmeal
3 tbsp chopped sage leaves
8 chicken thighs or drumsticks, skinned
½ cup low fat fromage frais
1 tsp whole-grain mustard
salt and black pepper
fresh sage leaves, to garnish

1 Preheat the oven to 400°F. Mix together the milk and plain mustard.

2 Mix the oatmeal with 2 tbsp of the sage and the seasoning on a plate. Brush the chicken with the milk and press into the oatmeal to coat.

3 Place the chicken on a baking sheet and bake for about 40 minutes, or until the juices run clear, not pink, when pierced through the thickest part.

4 Meanwhile, mix together the low fat fromage frais, mustard, remaining sage and seasoning, then serve with the chicken. Garnish the chicken with fresh sage and serve hot or cold.

COOK'S TIP
If fresh sage is not available, choose another fresh herb such as thyme or parsley, instead of using a dried alternative.

NUTRITION NOTES

Per portion:

Energy	214Kcals/898kJ
Fat	6.57g
Saturated fat	1.81g
Cholesterol	64.64mg
Fiber	0.74g

CHICKEN IN CREAMY ORANGE SAUCE

This sauce is deceptively creamy – in fact it is made with low fat fromage frais, which is virtually fat-free. The brandy adds a richer flavor, but is optional – omit it if you prefer and use orange juice alone.

INGREDIENTS

Serves 4
8 chicken thighs or drumsticks, skinned
3 tbsp brandy
1¼ cups orange juice
3 scallions, chopped
2 tsp cornstarch
6 tbsp low fat fromage frais
salt and black pepper

1 Cook the chicken pieces without fat in a nonstick or heavy pan, turning until evenly browned.

2 Stir in the brandy, orange juice and scallions. Bring to a boil, then cover and simmer for 15 minutes, or until the chicken is tender and the juices run clear, not pink, when pierced.

3 Blend the cornstarch with a little water then mix into the fromage frais. Stir this into the sauce and stir over moderate heat until boiling.

4 Adjust the seasoning and serve with boiled rice or pasta and green salad.

> **COOK'S TIP**
> Cornstarch stabilizes the fromage frais and helps prevent it curdling.

NUTRITION NOTES

Per portion:

Energy	227Kcals/951kJ
Fat	6.77g
Saturated fat	2.23g
Cholesterol	87.83mg
Fiber	0.17g

MANDARIN SESAME DUCK

Duck is a high-fat meat but it is possible to get rid of a good proportion of the fat cooked in this way. (If you remove the skin completely, the meat can be dry.) For a special occasion, duck breasts are a good choice, but they are more expensive.

INGREDIENTS

Serves 4
4 duck legs or boneless breasts
2 tbsp light soy sauce
3 tbsp clear honey
1 tbsp sesame seeds
4 mandarin oranges or tangerines
1 tsp cornstarch
salt and black pepper

1 Preheat the oven to 180°C/350°F/ Gas 4. Prick the duck skin all over. Slash the breast skin diagonally at intervals with a sharp knife.

2 Place the duck on a rack in a roasting pan and roast for 1 hour. Mix 1 tbsp soy sauce with 2 tbsp honey and brush over the duck. Sprinkle with sesame seeds. Roast for 15–20 minutes, until golden brown.

3 Meanwhile, grate the rind from one mandarin and squeeze the juice from two. Mix in the cornstarch, then stir in the remaining soy sauce and honey. Heat, stirring, until thickened and clear. Season. Peel and slice the remaining mandarins. Serve the duck, with the mandarin slices and the sauce.

NUTRITION NOTES

Per portion:
Energy	624Kcals/2621kJ
Fat	48.63g
Saturated fat	12.99g
Cholesterol	256mg
Fiber	0.95g

MINTY YOGURT CHICKEN

INGREDIENTS

Serves 4
8 chicken thighs, skinned
1 tbsp clear honey
2 tbsp lime or lemon juice
2 tbsp plain yogurt
4 tbsp chopped fresh mint
salt and black pepper

1 Slash the chicken flesh at intervals with a sharp knife. Place in a bowl.

2 Mix the lime or honey, lemon juice, yogurt, seasoning and half the mint.

3 Spoon the marinade over the chicken and leave to marinate for 30 minutes. Line a broiler pan with foil and cook the chicken under a broiler until thoroughly cooked and golden brown, turning the chicken occasionally during cooking.

4 Sprinkle with the remaining mint. Serve with potatoes and tomato salad.

NUTRITION NOTES

Per portion:
Energy	171Kcals/719kJ
Fat	6.74g
Saturated fat	2.23g
Cholesterol	97.90mg
Fiber	0.01g

PHEASANT WITH APPLES

Pheasant is worth buying as it is low in fat, full of flavor, and never dry when cooked like this.

INGREDIENTS

Serves 4
1 pheasant
2 small onions, quartered
3 celery stalks, thickly sliced
2 red eating apples, thickly sliced
½ cup broth
1 tbsp clear honey
2 tbsp Worcestershire sauce
ground nutmeg
2 tbsp toasted hazelnuts
salt and black pepper

1 Preheat the oven to 350°F. Sauté the pheasant without fat in a nonstick pan, turning occasionally until golden. Remove and keep hot.

2 Sauté the onions and celery in the pan to brown lightly. Spoon into a casserole and place the pheasant on top. Tuck the apple slices around it.

3 Spoon over the broth, honey, and Worcestershire sauce. Sprinkle with nutmeg, salt and pepper, cover, and bake for 1¼–1½ hours or until tender. Sprinkle with nuts and serve hot.

NUTRITION NOTES

Per portion:
Energy	387Kcals/1624kJ
Fat	16.97g
Saturated fat	4.28g
Cholesterol	126mg
Fiber	2.72g

CIDER BAKED RABBIT

Rabbit is a low fat meat and an economical choice for family meals. Chicken pieces may be used as an alternative.

INGREDIENTS

Serves 4
1 lb rabbit pieces
1 tbsp all-purpose flour
1 tsp dry mustard
3 medium leeks, thickly sliced
1 cup dry cider
2 sprigs rosemary
salt and black pepper
fresh rosemary, to garnish

1 Preheat the oven to 350°F. Place the rabbit pieces in a bowl and sprinkle over the flour and mustard. Toss to coat evenly.

2 Arrange the rabbit in one layer in a wide casserole. Blanch the leeks in boiling water, then drain and add to the casserole.

3 Add the cider, rosemary, and seasoning, cover, then bake for 1–1¼ hours, or until the rabbit is tender. Garnish with fresh rosemary, and serve with baked potatoes and vegetables.

NUTRITION NOTES

Per portion:
Energy	162Kcals/681kJ
Fat	4.22g
Saturated fat	1.39g
Cholesterol	62.13mg
Fiber	1.27g

FISH AND SEAFOOD

F ish is ideally designed for healthy, quick family meals. Most types of fish are very low in fat and high in protein, and even oily fish is high in essential fatty acids. Unlike meat, fish never needs long, slow cooking to tenderize it, so dinner can be on the table in less than half an hour! Tempt reluctant fish eaters with wonderful exotic flavors – a spicy Moroccan Fish Tagine perhaps, or a hearty Cod Creole to pep up the taste buds. Fussy young fish-eaters are sure to clean their plate of Fish Balls in Tomato Sauce or Tuna and Corn Fish Cakes, or will even try mackerel if it is presented without risk of bones, on fun-to-eat kabobs.

FISH BALLS IN TOMATO SAUCE

This quick meal is a good choice for young children, as you can guarantee no bones. If you like, add a dash of chili sauce.

INGREDIENTS

Serves 4

1 lb white fish fillets such as cod or flounder, skinned
4 tbsp fresh whole-wheat bread crumbs
2 tbsp snipped chives or scallions
14oz can chopped tomatoes
¾ cup button mushrooms, sliced
salt and black pepper

1 Cut the fish fillets into large chunks and place in a food processor. Add the whole-wheat bread crumbs and chives or scallions. Season to taste with salt and pepper, and process until the fish is finely chopped but still has some texture left.

2 Divide the fish mixture into about 16 even-sized pieces, then shape them into balls with your hands.

3 Place the tomatoes and mushrooms in a wide saucepan and cook over medium heat until boiling. Add the fish balls, cover and simmer for about 10 minutes, until cooked. Serve hot.

COOK'S TIP
The fish balls can be prepared several hours in advance if covered and kept in the refrigerator.

NUTRITION NOTES

Per portion:

Energy	138Kcals/580kJ
Fat	1.38g
Saturated fat	0.24g
Cholesterol	51.75mg
Fiber	1.89g

TUNA AND CORN FISH CAKES

These economical little tuna fish cakes are quick to make. Either use fresh mashed potatoes, or make a less fussy version with instant mashed potatoes.

INGREDIENTS

Serves 4

1¼ cups cooked mashed
  potatoes
7oz can tuna in vegetable oil,
  drained
¾ cup canned or frozen corn
  kernels
2 tbsp chopped fresh parsley
1 cup fresh white or whole-wheat
  bread crumbs
salt and black pepper
lemon wedges, to serve

1 Place the mashed potato in a bowl and stir in the tuna, corn kernels, and chopped parsley.

2 Season to taste with salt and pepper, then shape into eight patty shapes with your hands.

3 Spread out the bread crumbs on a plate and press the fish cakes into the bread crumbs to coat lightly, then place on a baking sheet.

4 Cook the fish cakes under a moderately hot broiler until crisp and golden brown, turning once. Serve hot, with lemon wedges and fresh vegetables.

COOK'S TIP
For simple variations that are just as pleasing and nutritious, try using canned sardines, red or pink salmon, or smoked mackerel in place of the tuna.

NUTRITION NOTES

Per portion:

Energy	203Kcals/852kJ
Fat	4.62g
Saturated fat	0.81g
Cholesterol	21.25mg
Fiber	1.82g

CRUNCHY-TOPPED COD

Colorful and quick to cook, this is ideal for weekday meals.

———— INGREDIENTS ————

Serves 4
4 pieces cod fillet, about 4oz each, skinned
2 medium tomatoes, sliced
1 cup fresh whole-wheat bread crumbs
2 tbsp chopped fresh parsley
finely grated rind and juice of ½ lemon
1 tsp sunflower oil
salt and black pepper

1 Preheat the oven to 400°F. Arrange the cod fillets in a wide, ovenproof dish.

2 Arrange the tomato slices on top. Mix together the bread crumbs, fresh parsley, lemon rind and juice, and the oil with seasoning to taste.

3 Spoon the crumb mixture evenly over the fish, then bake for 15–20 minutes. Serve hot.

—— NUTRITION NOTES ——

Per portion:

Energy	130Kcals/546kJ
Fat	2.06g
Saturated fat	0.32g
Cholesterol	52.9mg
Fiber	1.4g

SPECIAL FISH PIE

This fish pie is colorful, healthy, and best of all very easy to make. For a more economical version, omit the shrimp and replace with more fish fillet.

———— INGREDIENTS ————

Serves 4
12oz haddock fillet, skinned
2 tbsp cornstarch
4oz cooked, peeled shrimp
7oz can corn kernels, drained
¾ cup frozen peas
⅔ cup skim milk
⅔ cup low fat fromage frais
1½ cups fresh whole-wheat bread crumbs
½ cup shredded low fat Cheddar cheese
salt and black pepper

1 Preheat the oven to 375°F. Cut the haddock into bite-sized pieces and toss in cornstarch.

2 Place the fish, shrimp, corn, and peas in an ovenproof dish. Beat together the milk, fromage frais, and seasonings, then pour into the dish.

3 Mix together the bread crumbs and shredded cheese, then spoon evenly over the top. Bake for 25–30 minutes, or until golden brown. Serve hot, with fresh vegetables.

—— NUTRITION NOTES ——

Per portion:

Energy	290Kcals/1218kJ
Fat	4.87g
Saturated fat	2.1g
Cholesterol	63.91mg
Fiber	2.61g

HADDOCK AND BROCCOLI CHOWDER

A warming main-meal soup for hearty appetites.

INGREDIENTS

Serves 4

4 scallions, sliced
1 lb new potatoes, diced
1¼ cups fish broth or water
1¼ cups skim milk
1 bay leaf
2 cups broccoli florets, sliced
1 lb smoked haddock fillets, skinned
7oz can corn kernels, drained
black pepper
chopped scallions, to garnish

1 Place the scallions and potatoes in a large saucepan and add the broth, milk, and bay leaf. Bring the soup to a boil, then cover the pan and simmer for 10 minutes.

2 Add the broccoli to the pan. Cut the fish into bite-sized chunks and add to the pan with the corn kernels.

3 Season the soup well with black pepper, then cover the pan and simmer for 5 minutes more, or until the fish is cooked through. Remove the bay leaf and scatter over the scallions. Serve hot, with crusty bread.

COOK'S TIP
When new potatoes are not available, old ones can be used, but choose a waxy variety that will not disintegrate.

NUTRITION NOTES

Per portion:

Energy	268Kcals/1124kJ
Fat	2.19g
Saturated fat	0.27g
Cholesterol	57.75mg
Fiber	3.36g

MOROCCAN FISH TAGINE

Tagine is actually the name of the large Moroccan cooking pot used for this type of cooking, but you can use an ordinary casserole intead.

INGREDIENTS

Serves 4

2 garlic cloves, crushed
2 tbsp ground cumin
2 tbsp paprika
1 small red chili (optional)
2 tbsp tomato paste
4 tbsp lemon juice
4 whiting or cod steaks, about 6oz each
12oz tomatoes, sliced
2 green bell peppers, seeded and
    thinly sliced
salt and black pepper
chopped fresh cilantro, to garnish

1 Mix together the garlic, cumin, paprika, chili, tomato paste and lemon juice. Spread this mixture over the fish, then cover and chill for about 30 minutes to let the flavor penetrate.

2 Preheat the oven to 400°F. Arrange half of the tomatoes and peppers in a baking dish.

3 Cover with the fish, in one layer, then arrange the remaining tomatoes and bell pepper on top. Cover the baking dish with foil and bake for about 45 minutes, until the fish is cooked through. Sprinkle with chopped cilantro and serve.

COOK'S TIP
If you are preparing this dish for a dinner party, it can be assembled completely and stored in the fridge, ready for baking when needed.

NUTRITION NOTES

Per portion:
Energy	203Kcals/855kJ
Fat	3.34g
Saturated fat	0.29g
Cholesterol	80.5mg
Fiber	2.48g

SEAFOOD PILAF

This all-in-one-pan main course is a satisfying meal for any day of the week. For a special meal, substitute dry white wine for the orange juice.

INGREDIENTS

Serves 4
2 tsp olive oil
1¼ cups long-grain rice
1 tsp ground turmeric
1 red bell pepper, seeded and diced
1 small onion, finely chopped
2 medium zucchini, sliced
2 cups button mushrooms, halved
1½ cups fish or chicken broth
⅔ cup orange juice
12oz white fish fillets
12 fresh mussels in the shell (or cooked shelled mussels)
salt and ground black pepper
grated rind of 1 orange, to garnish

1 Heat the oil in a large, nonstick pan and sauté the rice and turmeric over low heat for about 1 minute.

2 Add the pepper, onion, zucchini, and mushrooms. Stir in the broth and orange juice. Bring to a boil.

3 Reduce the heat and add the fish. Cover and simmer gently for about 15 minutes, until the rice is tender and the liquid absorbed. Stir in the mussels and heat thoroughly. Adjust the seasoning, sprinkle with orange rind, and serve hot.

NUTRITION NOTES

Per portion:

Energy	370Kcals/1555kJ
Fat	3.84g
Saturated fat	0.64g
Cholesterol	61.25mg
Fiber	2.08g

SALMON PASTA WITH PARSLEY SAUCE

INGREDIENTS

Serves 4
1 lb salmon fillet, skinned
3 cups pasta, such as penne or twists
6oz cherry tomatoes, halved
⅔ cup low fat crème fraîche
3 tbsp finely chopped parsley
finely grated rind of ½ orange
salt and black pepper

NUTRITION NOTES

Per portion:

Energy	452Kcals/1902kJ
Fat	17.4g
Saturated fat	5.36g
Cholesterol	65.63mg
Fiber	2.56g

1 Cut the salmon into bite-sized pieces, arrange on a heatproof plate, and cover with foil.

2 Bring a large pan of salted water to the boil, add the pasta, and return to a boil. Place the plate of salmon on top and simmer for 10–12 minutes, until the pasta and salmon are cooked.

3 Drain the pasta and toss with the tomatoes and salmon. Mix together the crème fraîche, parsley, orange rind, and pepper to taste, then toss into the salmon and pasta and serve hot or cold.

STUFFED SOLE ROLLS

Sole fillets are a good choice because they are mild in flavor, easy to cook, and free of bones. Have your fillets prepared when you buy them.

INGREDIENTS

Serves 4
1 medium zucchini, grated
2 medium carrots, grated
4 tbsp fresh whole-wheat bread
  crumbs
1 tbsp lime or lemon juice
4 sole fillets
salt and black pepper

1 Preheat the oven to 400°F. Mix together the grated carrots and zucchini. Stir in the bread crumbs, lime juice, and seasoning to taste.

2 Lay the fish fillets skin side up and divide the stuffing between them, spreading it evenly.

3 Roll up to enclose the stuffing and place in an ovenproof dish. Cover and bake for about 30 minutes, or until the fish flakes easily. Serve hot with new potatoes.

COOK'S TIP
This recipe creates its own delicious juices, but for an extra sauce, stir chopped fresh parsley into a little low fat fromage frais and serve with the fish.

NUTRITION NOTES

Per portion:
Energy	158Kcals/665kJ
Fat	3.22g
Saturated fat	0.56g
Cholesterol	50.4mg
Fiber	1.94g

MACKEREL KABOBS WITH PARSLEY DRESSING

Oily fish such as mackerel are ideal for broiling as they cook quickly and need no extra oil.

INGREDIENTS

Serves 4
1 lb mackerel fillets
finely grated rind and juice of 1 lemon
3 tbsp chopped fresh parsley
12 cherry tomatoes
8 pitted ripe olives
salt and black pepper

1 Cut the fish into 1½in chunks and place in a bowl with half the lemon rind and juice, half of the parsley and some seasoning. Cover the bowl and leave to marinate for 30 minutes.

2 Thread the chunks of fish onto eight long wooden or metal skewers, alternating them with the cherry tomatoes and olives. Cook the kabobs under a hot broiler for 3–4 minutes, turning the kabobs occasionally, until the fish is cooked.

3 Mix the remaining lemon rind and juice with the remaining parsley in a small bowl, then season to taste with salt and pepper. Spoon the dressing over the kabobs and serve hot, with plain boiled rice or noodles and a leafy green salad.

COOK'S TIP
When using wooden or bamboo kabob skewers, soak them first in a bowl of cold water for a few minutes to help prevent them burning.

NUTRITION NOTES

Per portion:
Energy	268Kcals/1126kJ
Fat	19.27g
Saturated fat	4.5g
Cholesterol	61.88mg
Fiber	1g

HERRINGS WITH RED SALSA

Herrings are one of the most economical and nutritious fish. If you buy them ready filleted, they're much easier to eat than the whole fish.

INGREDIENTS

Serves 4
2 tbsp skim milk
2 tsp Dijon mustard
2 large herrings, filletted
⅔ cup oatmeal
salt and black pepper

For the salsa
1 small red bell pepper, seeded
4 medium tomatoes
1 scallion, chopped
1 tbsp lime juice
1 tsp granulated sugar

1 Preheat the oven to 400°F. To make the salsa, place the pepper, tomatoes, scallion, lime juice, sugar, and seasoning in a food processor. Process until finely chopped.

2 Mix the milk and mustard, and the oatmeal, and pepper. Dip fillets into the milk mixture, then oatmeal to coat.

3 Place on a baking sheet, then bake for 20 minutes. Serve with the salsa.

NUTRITION NOTES

Per portion:
Energy	261Kcals/1097kJ
Fat	15.56g
Saturated fat	3.17g
Cholesterol	52.65mg
Fiber	2.21g

SPICED RAINBOW TROUT

Farmed rainbow trout are very good value and cook very quickly under a broiler or on a barbecue. Herring and mackerel can be cooked in this way too.

INGREDIENTS

Serves 4
4 large rainbow trout fillets (about 5oz each)
1 tbsp ground coriander
1 garlic clove, crushed
2 tbsp finely chopped fresh mint
1 tsp paprika
¾ cup plain yogurt
salad and pita bread, to serve

1 With a sharp knife, slash the flesh of the fish fillets through the skin fairly deeply at intervals.

2 Mix together the coriander, garlic, mint, paprika, and yogurt. Spread this mixture evenly over the fish and leave to marinate for about 1 hour.

3 Cook the fish under a moderately hot broiler or on a barbecue, turning occasionally, until crisp and golden. Serve hot, with a crisp salad and some warmed pita bread.

COOK'S TIP
If you are using the broiler, it is best to line the pan with foil before cooking the trout.

NUTRITION NOTES

Per portion:
Energy	188Kcals/792kJ
Fat	5.66g
Saturated fat	1.45g
Cholesterol	110.87mg
Fiber	0.05g

Cod Creole

Serves 4

1 lb cod fillets, skinned
1 tbsp lime or lemon juice
2 tsp olive oil
1 medium onion, finely chopped
1 green bell pepper, seeded and sliced
½ tsp cayenne pepper
½ tsp garlic salt
14oz can chopped tomatoes

—— Nutrition Notes ——	
Per portion:	
Energy	130Kcals/546kJ
Fat	2.61g
Saturated fat	0.38g
Cholesterol	51.75mg
Fiber	1.61g

1 Cut the cod fillets into bite-sized chunks and sprinkle with the lime or lemon juice.

2 In a large, nonstick pan, heat the olive oil and sauté the onion and pepper gently until softened. Add the cayenne pepper and garlic salt.

3 Stir in the cod with the chopped tomatoes. Bring to a boil, then cover and simmer for about 5 minutes, or until the fish flakes easily. Serve with boiled rice or potatoes.

Five-Spice Fish

Chinese mixtures of spicy, sweet, and sour flavors are particularly successful with fish, and dinner is ready in minutes.

Serves 4

4 white fish fillets, such as cod, haddock
*   or flounder (about 6oz each)*
1 tsp Chinese five-spice powder
4 tsp cornstarch
1 tbsp sesame or sunflower oil
3 scallions, shredded
1 tsp finely chopped ginger
5oz button mushrooms, sliced
4oz baby corn, sliced
2 tbsp soy sauce
3 tbsp dry sherry or apple juice
1 tsp sugar
salt and black pepper

1 Toss the fish in the five-spice powder and cornstarch to coat.

2 Heat the oil in a frying pan or wok and stir-fry the scallions, ginger, mushrooms, and corn for about 1 minute. Add the fish and cook for 2–3 minutes, turning once.

3 Mix together the soy sauce, sherry, and sugar, then pour over the fish. Simmer for 2 minutes, adjust the seasoning, then serve with noodles and stir-fried vegetables.

—— Nutrition Notes ——	
Per portion:	
Energy	213Kcals/893kJ
Fat	4.41g
Saturated fat	0.67g
Cholesterol	80.5mg
Fiber	1.08g

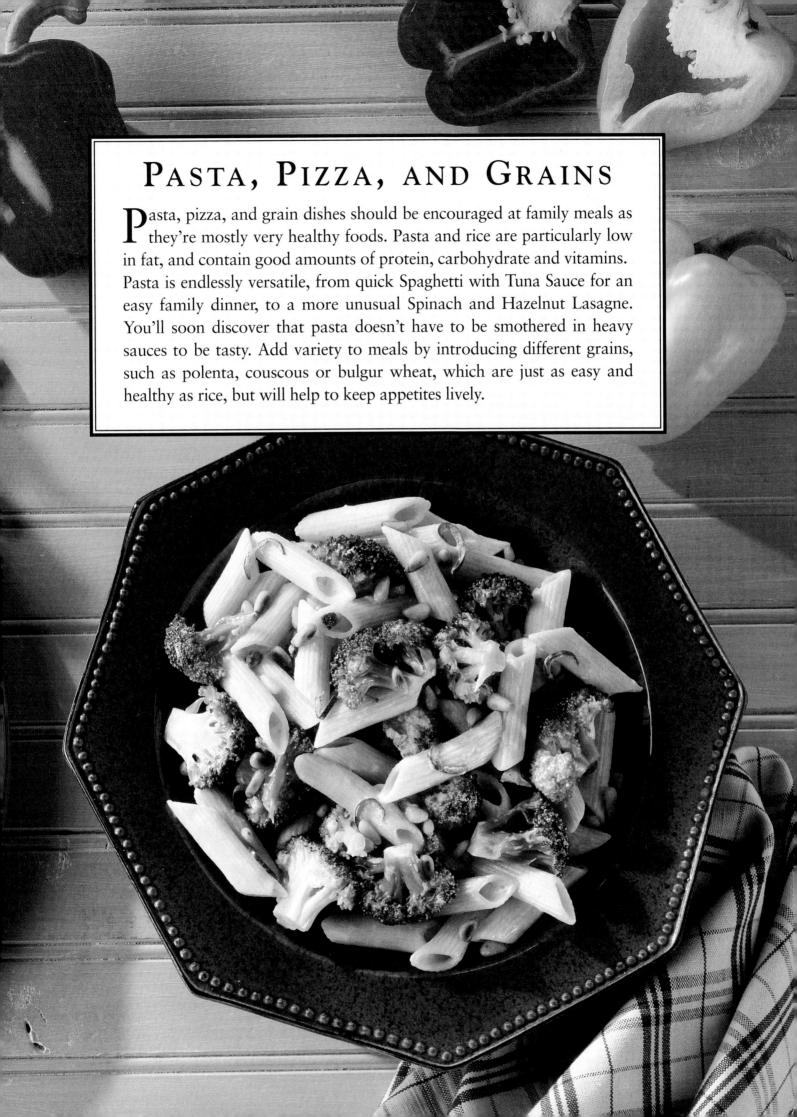

PASTA, PIZZA, AND GRAINS

Pasta, pizza, and grain dishes should be encouraged at family meals as they're mostly very healthy foods. Pasta and rice are particularly low in fat, and contain good amounts of protein, carbohydrate and vitamins. Pasta is endlessly versatile, from quick Spaghetti with Tuna Sauce for an easy family dinner, to a more unusual Spinach and Hazelnut Lasagne. You'll soon discover that pasta doesn't have to be smothered in heavy sauces to be tasty. Add variety to meals by introducing different grains, such as polenta, couscous or bulgur wheat, which are just as easy and healthy as rice, but will help to keep appetites lively.

LEMON AND HERB RISOTTO CAKE

This unusual rice dish can be served as a main course with salad, or as a satisfying side dish. It's also good served cold, and packs well for picnics.

INGREDIENTS

Serves 4
1 small leek, thinly sliced
2½ cups chicken broth
1 cup short-grain rice
finely grated rind of 1 lemon
2 tbsp chopped fresh chives
2 tbsp chopped fresh parsley
¾ cup shredded mozzarella cheese
salt and black pepper
parsley and lemon wedges, to garnish

1 Preheat the oven to 400°F. Lightly oil a deep-sided 8½ in round, loose-bottomed cake pan.

2 Cook the leek in a large pan with 3 tbsp broth, stirring over moderate heat, to soften. Add the rice and the remaining broth.

3 Bring to a boil. Cover the pan and simmer gently, stirring occasionally, for about 20 minutes, or until all the liquid is absorbed.

4 Stir in the lemon rind, herbs, cheese, and seasoning. Spoon into the cake pan, cover with foil and bake for 30–35 minutes or until lightly browned. Turn out and serve in slices, garnished with parsley and lemon wedges.

> **COOK'S TIP**
> The best type of rice to choose for this recipe is the Italian round grain Arborio rice, which should not be rinsed before use.

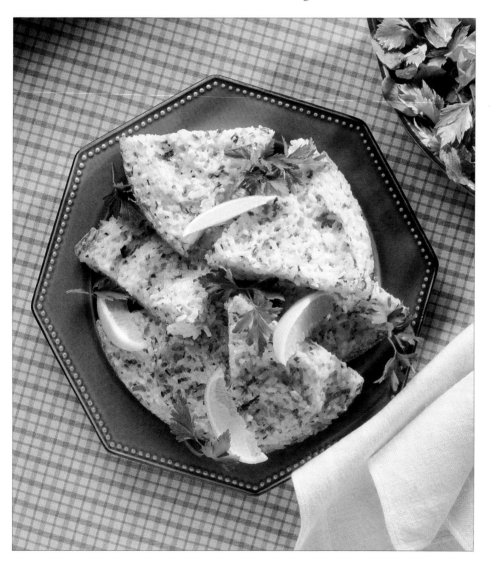

NUTRITION NOTES

Per portion:	
Energy	280Kcals/1176kJ
Fat	6.19g
Saturated fat	2.54g
Cholesterol	12.19mg
Fiber	0.9g

RICE WITH SEEDS AND SPICES

A change from plain boiled rice, and a colorful accompaniment to serve with spicy curries or broiled meats. Basmati rice gives the best texture and flavor, but you can use ordinary long-grain rice instead, if you prefer.

INGREDIENTS

Serves 4

1 tsp sunflower oil
½ tsp ground turmeric
6 cardamom pods, lightly crushed
1 tsp coriander seeds, lightly crushed
1 garlic clove, crushed
1 cup basmati rice
1⅔ cups broth
½ cup plain yogurt
1 tbsp toasted sunflower seeds
1 tbsp toasted sesame seeds
salt and black pepper
cilantro leaves, to garnish

1 Heat the oil in a nonstick pan and sauté the spices and garlic for about 1 minute, stirring all the time.

2 Add the rice and broth, bring to a boil, then cover and simmer for 15 minutes, or until just tender.

3 Stir in the yogurt and the toasted sunflower and sesame seeds. Adjust the seasoning and serve hot, garnished with cilantro leaves.

NUTRITION NOTES

Per portion:

Energy	243Kcals/1022kJ
Fat	5.5g
Saturated fat	0.73g
Cholesterol	1.15mg
Fiber	0.57g

COOK'S TIP
Seeds are particularly rich in minerals, so they are a good addition to all kinds of dishes. Light roasting will improve their flavor.

CORN KERNEL PANCAKES

These crisp pancakes are delicious to serve as a snack lunch, or as a light supper with a crisp mixed salad.

─── INGREDIENTS ───

Serves 4, makes about 12
1 cup self-rising flour
1 egg white
⅔ cup skim milk
7oz can corn kernels, drained
oil, for brushing
salt and black pepper
tomato chutney, to serve

1 Place the flour, egg white, and skim milk in a food processor or blender with half the corn and process until smooth.

2 Season the batter well and add the remaining corn.

3 Heat a frying pan and brush with oil. Drop in tablespoons of batter and cook until set. Turn over the pancakes and cook the other side until golden. Serve hot with tomato chutney.

─── NUTRITION NOTES ───

Per portion:
Energy	162Kcals/680kJ
Fat	0.89g
Saturated fat	0.14g
Cholesterol	0.75mg
Fiber	1.49g

BAKED POLENTA WITH TOMATOES

─── INGREDIENTS ───

Serves 4
3⅔ cups broth
scant 1¼ cups polenta (coarse corn-meal)
4 tbsp chopped fresh sage
1 tsp olive oil
2 beefsteak tomatoes, sliced
1 tbsp grated Parmesan cheese
salt and black pepper

1 Bring the broth to a boil in a large saucepan, then gradually stir in the polenta.

2 Continue stirring the polenta over moderate heat for about 5 minutes, until the mixture begins to come away from the sides of the pan. Stir in the chopped sage and season well, then spoon the polenta into a lightly oiled, shallow 9x13 in pan and spread evenly. Leave to cool.

3 Preheat the oven to 400°F. Cut the cooled polenta into 24 squares using a sharp knife.

4 Arrange the polenta overlapping with tomato slices in a lightly oiled, shallow ovenproof dish. Sprinkle with Parmesan and bake for 20 minutes, or until golden brown. Serve hot.

─── NUTRITION NOTES ───

Per portion:
Energy	200Kcals/842kJ
Fat	3.8g
Saturated fat	0.77g
Cholesterol	1.88mg
Fiber	1.71g

BULGUR AND LENTIL PILAF

Bulgur wheat is very easy to cook and can be used in almost any way you would normally use rice, hot or cold. Some of the finer grades need hardly any cooking, so check the package for cooking times.

INGREDIENTS

Serves 4
1 tsp olive oil
1 large onion, thinly sliced
2 garlic cloves, crushed
1 tsp ground coriander
1 tsp ground cumin
1 tsp ground turmeric
½ tsp ground allspice
1¼ cups bulgur wheat
about 3⅔ cups broth or water
1½ cups button mushrooms, sliced
⅔ cup green lentils
salt, black pepper and cayenne

1 Heat the oil in a nonstick saucepan and sauté the onion, garlic, and spices for 1 minute, stirring.

2 Stir in the bulgur wheat and cook, stirring, for about 2 minutes, until lightly browned. Add the broth or water, mushrooms, and lentils.

3 Simmer over very low heat for about 25–30 minutes, until the bulgur wheat and lentils are tender and all the liquid is absorbed. Add more broth or water, if necessary.

4 Season well with salt, pepper, and cayenne and serve hot.

COOK'S TIP
Green lentils can be cooked without presoaking, as they cook quite quickly and keep their shape. However, if you have the time, soaking them first will shorten the cooking time slightly.

NUTRITION NOTES

Per portion:
Energy	325Kcals/1367kJ
Fat	2.8g
Saturated fat	0.33g
Cholesterol	0
Fiber	3.61g

MINTED COUSCOUS CASTLES

Couscous is a fine semolina flour made from wheat grain, which is usually steamed and served plain with a rich meat or vegetable stew. Here it is flavored with mint and molded to make an unusual accompaniment to serve with any savory dish.

INGREDIENTS

Serves 6

1¼ cups couscous
2 cups boiling broth
1 tbsp lemon juice
2 tomatoes, diced
2 tbsp chopped fresh mint
oil, for brushing
salt and black pepper
mint sprigs, to garnish

1 Place the couscous in a bowl and pour over the boiling broth. Cover the bowl and leave to stand for 30 minutes, until all the broth is absorbed and the grains are tender.

2 Stir in the lemon juice with the tomatoes and chopped mint. Adjust the seasoning with salt and pepper.

3 Brush the insides of four cups or individual molds with oil. Spoon in the couscous mixture and pack down firmly. Chill for several hours.

4 Turn out and serve cold, or alternatively, cover and heat gently in a low oven or microwave, then turn out and serve hot, garnished with mint.

COOK'S TIP
Most couscous is now the ready-cooked variety, which can be cooked as above, but some types need steaming first, so check the package instructions.

NUTRITION NOTES

Per portion:

Energy	95Kcals/397kJ
Fat	0.53g
Saturated fat	0.07g
Cholesterol	0
Fiber	0.29g

TAGLIATELLE WITH HAZELNUT PESTO

Hazelnuts are lower in fat than other nuts, which makes them useful for this reduced-fat alternative to pesto sauce.

INGREDIENTS

Serves 4
2 garlic cloves, crushed
1 cup fresh basil leaves
¼ cup hazelnuts
⅞ cup skim milk soft cheese
8oz dried tagliatelle, or 1 lb fresh
salt and black pepper

1 Place the garlic, basil, hazelnuts, and cheese in a food processor or blender and process to a thick paste.

2 Cook the tagliatelle in lightly salted boiling water until just tender, then drain well.

3 Spoon the sauce into the hot pasta, tossing until melted. Sprinkle with pepper and serve hot.

NUTRITION NOTES	
Per portion:	
Energy	274Kcals/1155kJ
Fat	5.05g
Saturated fat	0.43g
Cholesterol	0.5mg
Fiber	2.14g

SPAGHETTI WITH TUNA SAUCE

A speedy mid-week meal, which can also be made with other pasta shapes.

INGREDIENTS

Serves 4
8oz dried spaghetti, or 1 lb fresh
1 garlic clove, crushed
14oz can chopped tomatoes
15oz can tuna in water, flaked
½ tsp chili sauce (optional)
4 pitted ripe olives, chopped
salt and black pepper

1 Cook the spaghetti in lightly salted boiling water for 12 minutes or until just tender. Drain well and keep hot.

2 Add the garlic and tomatoes to the saucepan and bring to a boil. Simmer, uncovered, for 2–3 minutes.

3 Add the tuna, chili sauce, if using, olives, and spaghetti. Heat well, add the seasoning, and serve hot.

COOK'S TIP
If fresh tuna is available, use 1lb, cut into small chunks, and add after step 2. Simmer for 6–8 minutes, then add the chili sauce, olives, and pasta.

NUTRITION NOTES	
Per portion:	
Energy	306Kcals/1288kJ
Fat	2.02g
Saturated fat	0.37g
Cholesterol	48.45mg
Fiber	2.46g

SPINACH AND HAZELNUT LASAGNE

A vegetarian dish that is hearty enough to satisfy meat-eaters too. Use frozen spinach if you're short of time.

INGREDIENTS

Serves 4

2 lb fresh spinach
1¼ cups vegetable or chicken broth
1 medium onion, finely chopped
1 garlic clove, crushed
¾ cup hazelnuts
2 tbsp chopped fresh basil
6 sheets lasagne
14oz can chopped tomatoes
1 cup low fat fromage frais
slivered hazlenuts and chopped parsley,
    to garnish

1 Preheat the oven to 400°F. Wash the spinach and place in a pan with just the water that clings to the leaves. Cook the spinach over a fairly high heat for 2 minutes until wilted. Drain well.

2 Heat 2 tbsp of the broth in a large pan and simmer the onion and garlic until soft. Stir in the spinach, hazelnuts, and basil.

3 In a large ovenproof dish, layer the spinach, lasagne, and tomatoes. Season well between the layers. Pour over the remaining broth. Spread the fromage frais over the top.

4 Bake the lasagne for about 45 minutes, or until golden brown. Serve hot, sprinkled with lines of slivered hazelnuts and chopped parsley.

COOK'S TIP
The flavor of hazelnuts is improved by roasting. Place them on a baking sheet and bake in a moderate oven, or under a hot broiler, until light golden.

NUTRITION NOTES

Per portion:

Energy	365Kcals/1532kJ
Fat	17g
Saturated fat	1.46g
Cholesterol	0.5mg
Fiber	8.16g

CALZONE

INGREDIENTS

Makes 4
4 cups flour
pinch of salt
1 envelope active dry yeast
about 1½ cups warm water

For the filling
1 tsp olive oil
1 medium red onion, thinly sliced
3 medium zucchini, about 12oz total
  weight, sliced
2 large tomatoes, diced
1 cup mozzarella cheese, diced
1 tbsp chopped fresh oregano
skim milk, to glaze
salt and black pepper

1 To make the dough, sift the flour and salt into a bowl and stir in the yeast. Stir in just enough warm water to mix to a soft dough.

2 Knead for 5 minutes until smooth. Cover and leave in a warm place for about 1 hour, or until doubled in size.

3 Meanwhile, to make the filling, heat the oil and sauté the onion and zucchini for 3–4 minutes. Remove from the heat and add the tomatoes, cheese, oregano, and seasoning.

4 Preheat the oven to 425°F. Knead the dough lightly and divide into four. Roll out each piece on a lightly floured surface to a 8in round, and place a quarter of the filling on one half.

5 Brush the edges with milk and fold over to enclose the filling. Press firmly to enclose. Brush with milk.

6 Bake on an oiled baking sheet for 15–20 minutes. Serve hot or cold.

NUTRITION NOTES	
Per portion:	
Energy	544Kcals/2285kJ
Fat	10.93g
Saturated fat	5.49g
Cholesterol	24.42mg
Fiber	5.09g

PENNE WITH BROCCOLI AND CHILI

INGREDIENTS

Serves 4

1 lb small broccoli florets
2 tbsp broth
1 garlic clove, crushed
1 small red chili pepper, sliced, or ½ tsp
   chili sauce
4 tbsp plain low fat yogurt
2 tbsp toasted pine nuts or cashews
3¾ cups penne pasta
salt and black pepper

1 Add the pasta to a large pan of lightly salted boiling water and return to a boil. Place the broccoli in a steamer basket over the top. Cover and cook for 8–10 minutes until both are just tender. Drain.

2 Heat the broth and add the crushed garlic and chili or chili sauce. Stir over low heat for 2–3 minutes.

3 Stir in the broccoli, pasta, and yogurt. Adjust the seasoning, sprinkle with nuts, and serve hot.

NUTRITION NOTES

Per portion:

Energy	403Kcals/1695kJ
Fat	7.87g
Saturated fat	0.89g
Cholesterol	0.6mg
Fiber	5.83g

CREOLE JAMBALAYA

INGREDIENTS

Serves 6

4 boneless chicken thighs, skinned and
   diced
1 large green bell pepper, seeded and
   sliced
3 celery stalks, sliced
4 scallions, sliced
about 1¼ cups chicken broth
14oz can tomatoes
1 tsp ground cumin
1 tsp ground allspice
½ tsp cayenne pepper
1 tsp dried thyme
1½ cups long-grain rice
7oz cooked, peeled shrimp
salt and black pepper

1 Brown the chicken in a nonstick pan without fat, turning occasionally, until golden all over.

2 Add the pepper, celery, and onions with 1 tbsp broth. Cook for a few minutes to soften, then add the tomatoes, spices, and thyme.

3 Stir in the rice and broth. Cover and cook for about 20 minutes, stirring occasionally, until the rice is tender. Add more broth if necessary.

4 Add the shrimp and heat well. Season and serve with a crisp salad.

NUTRITION NOTES

Per portion:

Energy	282Kcals/1185kJ
Fat	3.37g
Saturated fat	0.85g
Cholesterol	51.33mg
Fiber	1.55g

PASTA WITH CHICK PEA SAUCE

INGREDIENTS

Serves 4

2 cups pasta
1 tsp olive oil
1 small onion, finely chopped
1 garlic clove, crushed
1 celery stalk, finely chopped
15oz can chick peas, drained
1 cup tomato sauce
salt and black pepper
chopped fresh parsley, to garnish

1 Heat the olive oil in a nonstick pan and sauté the onion, garlic, and celery until softened, not browned. Stir in the chick peas and tomato sauce, then cover and simmer for about 15 minutes.

2 Cook the pasta in a large pan of boiling, lightly salted water until just tender. Drain the pasta and toss into the sauce, then season to taste with salt and pepper. Sprinkle with chopped fresh parsley, then serve hot.

NUTRITION NOTES

Per portion:
Energy	374Kcals/1570kJ
Fat	4.44g
Saturated fat	0.32g
Cholesterol	0
Fiber	6.41g

PEPERONATA PIZZA

INGREDIENTS

Makes 2 large pizzas

4 cups flour
pinch of salt
1 envelope active dry yeast
about 1½ cups warm water

For the topping
1 onion, sliced
2 tsp olive oil
2 large red and 2 yellow bell peppers,
  seeded and sliced
1 garlic clove, crushed
14oz can tomatoes
8 pitted ripe olives, halved
salt and black pepper

1 To make the dough, sift the flour and salt into a bowl and stir in the yeast. Stir in just enough warm water to mix to a soft dough.

2 Knead for 5 minutes until smooth. Cover and leave in a warm place for about 1 hour, or until doubled in size.

3 To make the topping, sauté the onion in the oil until soft, then stir in the peppers, garlic, and tomatoes. Cover and simmer for 30 minutes, until no liquid remains. Season to taste.

4 Preheat the oven to 450°F. Divide the dough in half and press out each piece on a lightly oiled baking sheet to a 11in round, turning up the edges slightly.

5 Spread over the topping, dot with olives, and bake for 15–20 minutes. Serve hot or cold, with salad.

NUTRITION NOTES

Per portion:
Energy	965Kcals/4052kJ
Fat	9.04g
Saturated fat	1.07g
Cholesterol	0
Fiber	14.51g

VEGETABLES AND SALADS

We're very lucky to have a huge variety of fresh vegetables available all year round these days, so there is no excuse for not making maximum use of them in every meal, whether they form the basis of the main course, or are served as an accompaniment to meat or fish dishes. Get out of that dull daily rut of the same old familiar vegetables and try pepping them up with unusual flavors – Brussels sprouts will never be the same again when you've cooked them Chinese-style, and if you thought roast potatoes were banned, try Rosemary Roasties. Take a fresh look at salads, too, and discover that they needn't be soaked in heavy, oily dressings. Tangy plain low fat yogurt dressings or mustard and honey mixtures are light, flavorful and low in fat.

Chinese Sprouts

If you are bored with plain boiled Brussels sprouts, try pepping them up with this unusual stir-fried method, which uses the minimum of oil.

Ingredients

Serves 4

1 lb Brussels sprouts, shredded
1 tsp sesame or sunflower oil
2 scallions, sliced
½ tsp Chinese five-spice powder
1 tbsp light soy sauce

1 Trim the Brussels sprouts, then shred them finely using a large sharp knife or shred in a food processor.

2 Heat the oil and add the sprouts and onions, then stir-fry for about 2 minutes, without browning.

3 Stir in the five-spice powder and soy sauce, then cook, stirring, for 2–3 minutes more, until just tender.

4 Serve hot, with broiled meats or fish, or Chinese dishes.

Cook's Tip
Brussels sprouts are rich in Vitamin C, and this is a good way to cook them to preserve the vitamins. Larger sprouts cook particularly well by this method, and cabbage can also be cooked this way.

Nutrition Notes

Per portion:

Energy	58Kcals/243kJ
Fat	2.38g
Saturated fat	0.26g
Cholesterol	0
Fiber	4.67g

LEMONY VEGETABLE PARCELS

INGREDIENTS

Serves 4
2 medium carrots
1 small rutabaga
1 large parsnip
1 leek, sliced
finely grated rind of ½ lemon
1 tbsp lemon juice
1 tbsp whole-grain mustard
1 tsp walnut or sunflower oil
salt and black pepper

1 Preheat the oven to 375°F. Peel the root vegetables and cut into ½ in cubes. Place in a large bowl, then add the sliced leek.

2 Stir the lemon rind and juice and the mustard into the vegetables and mix well, then season to taste.

3 Cut four 12 in squares of nonstick baking paper and brush them lightly with the oil.

4 Divide the vegetables among them. Roll up the paper from one side, then twist the ends firmly to seal.

5 Place the parcels on a baking sheet and bake for 50–55 minutes, or until the vegetables are just tender. Serve hot, with roast or broiled meats.

NUTRITION NOTES	
Per portion	
Energy	78Kcals/326kJ
Fat	2.06g
Saturated fat	0.08g
Cholesterol	0
Fiber	5.15g

VEGETABLE RIBBONS

This may just tempt a few fussy eaters to eat up their vegetables!

INGREDIENTS

Serves 4
3 medium carrots
3 medium zucchini
½ cup chicken broth
2 tbsp chopped fresh parsley
salt and black pepper

1 Using a vegetable peeler or sharp knife, cut the carrots and zucchini into thin ribbons.

2 Bring the broth to a boil in a large saucepan and add the carrots. Return the broth to a boil, then add the zucchini. Boil rapidly for 2–3 minutes, or until the vegetable ribbons are just tender.

3 Stir in the parsley, season lightly, and serve hot.

NUTRITION NOTES

Per portion:

Energy	35Kcals/144kJ
Fat	0.53g
Saturated fat	0.09g
Cholesterol	0
Fiber	2.19g

VEGGIE BURGERS

INGREDIENTS

Serves 4
4oz cup mushrooms, finely chopped
1 small onion, chopped
1 small zucchini, chopped
1 carrot, chopped
1oz unsalted peanuts or cashews
2 cups fresh bread crumbs
2 tbsp chopped fresh parsley
1 tsp yeast extract
salt and black pepper
fine oatmeal or flour, for shaping

1 Cook the mushrooms in a nonstick pan without oil, stirring, for 8–10 minutes to remove all the moisture.

2 Process the onion, zucchini, carrot, and nuts in a food processor until beginning to bind together.

3 Stir in the mushrooms, bread-crumbs, parsley, yeast extract, and seasoning to taste. With the oatmeal or flour, shape into four burgers. Chill.

4 Cook the burgers in a nonstick frying pan with very little oil or under a hot broiler for 8–10 minutes, turning once, until the burgers are cooked and golden brown. Serve hot with a crisp salad.

NUTRITION NOTES

Per portion:

Energy	126Kcals/530kJ
Fat	3.8g
Saturated fat	0.73g
Cholesterol	0
Fiber	2.21g

MIDDLE-EASTERN VEGETABLE STEW

A spiced dish of mixed vegetables that can be served as a side dish or as a vegetarian main course. Children may prefer less chili.

INGREDIENTS

Serves 4–6

3 tbsp vegetable or chicken broth
1 green bell pepper, seeded and sliced
2 medium zucchini, sliced
2 medium carrots, sliced
2 celery sticks, sliced
2 medium potatoes, diced
14oz can chopped tomatoes
1 tsp chili powder
2 tbsp chopped fresh mint
1 tbsp ground cumin
14oz can chick peas, drained
salt and black pepper
mint sprigs, to garnish

1 Heat the vegetable or chicken broth in a large flameproof casserole until boiling, then add the sliced bell pepper, zucchini, carrot, and celery. Stir over high heat for 2–3 minutes, until the vegetables are just beginning to soften.

2 Add the potatoes, tomatoes, chili powder, mint, and cumin. Add the chick peas and bring to a boil.

3 Reduce the heat, cover the casserole, and simmer for 30 minutes, or until all the vegetables are tender. Season to taste with salt and pepper and serve hot, garnished with mint leaves.

COOK'S TIP
Chick peas are traditional in this type of Middle-Eastern dish, but if you prefer, red kidney beans or navy beans can be used instead.

NUTRITION NOTES

Per portion:

Energy	168Kcals/703kJ
Fat	3.16g
Saturated fat	0.12g
Cholesterol	0
Fiber	6.13g

SUMMER VEGETABLE BRAISE

Tender, young vegetables are ideal for quick cooking in a minimum of liquid. Use any mixture of the family's favorite vegetables, as long as they are of similar size.

INGREDIENTS

Serves 4
2½ cups baby carrots
2 cups sugar-snap peas or snow peas
1¼ cups baby corn
6 tbsp vegetable broth
2 tsp lime juice
salt and black pepper
chopped fresh parsley and snipped fresh
   chives, to garnish

1 Place the carrots, peas, and baby corn in a large heavy-based saucepan with the vegetable broth and lime juice. Bring to a boil.

2 Cover the pan and reduce the heat, then simmer for 6–8 minutes, shaking the pan occasionally, until the vegetables are just tender.

3 Season the vegetables to taste with salt and pepper, then stir in the chopped fresh parsley and snipped chives. Cook the vegetables for a few seconds more, stirring them once or twice until the herbs are well mixed, then serve at once, with broiled lamb chops or roast chicken.

COOK'S TIP
You can make this dish in the winter too, but cut larger, tougher vegetables into chunks and cook for slightly longer.

NUTRITION NOTES
Per portion:
Energy	36Kcals/152kJ
Fat	0.45g
Saturated fat	0
Cholesterol	0
Fiber	2.35g

Spicy Baked Potatoes

Ingredients

Serves 2–4

2 large baking potatoes
1 tsp sunflower oil
1 small onion, finely chopped
1in piece fresh ginger root, grated
1 tsp ground cumin
1 tsp ground coriander
½ tsp ground turmeric
garlic salt
plain yogurt and fresh cilantro sprigs,
to serve

1 Preheat the oven to 375°F. Prick the potatoes with a fork. Bake for 40 minutes, or until soft.

2 Cut the potatoes in half and scoop out the flesh. Heat the oil in a nonstick pan and sauté the onion for a few minutes to soften. Stir in the ginger, cumin, coriander, and turmeric.

3 Stir over low heat for about 2 minutes, then add the potato flesh, and garlic salt, to taste.

4 Cook the potato mixture for 2 minutes more, stirring occasionally. Spoon the mixture back into the potato shells and top each with a spoonful of plain yogurt and a sprig or two of fresh cilantro. Serve hot.

Nutrition Notes

Per portion:

Energy	212Kcals/890kJ
Fat	2.54g
Saturated fat	0.31g
Cholesterol	0.4mg
Fiber	3.35g

Two Beans Provençal

Ingredients

Serves 4

1 tsp olive oil
1 small onion, finely chopped
1 garlic clove, crushed
8oz haricot verts beans
8oz green beans
2 tomatoes, peeled and chopped
salt and black pepper

Nutrition Notes

Per portion:

Energy	68Kcals/286kJ
Fat	1.76g
Saturated fat	0.13g
Cholesterol	0
Fibre	5.39g

1 Heat the oil in a heavy-based, or nonstick, pan and sauté the chopped onion over medium heat until softened but not browned.

2 Add the garlic, both the beans, and the tomatoes, then season well and cover tightly.

3 Cook over fairly low heat, shaking the pan occasionally, for about 30 minutes, or until the beans are tender. Serve hot.

BROCCOLI-CAULIFLOWER GRATIN

Broccoli and cauliflower make
an attractive combination, and
this dish is much lighter than the
classic cheese sauce.

INGREDIENTS

Serves 4
1 small cauliflower (about 9oz)
1 small head broccoli (about 9oz)
½ cup plain low fat yogurt
*1 cup shredded low fat Cheddar
   cheese*
1 tsp whole-grain mustard
2 tbsp whole-wheat bread crumbs
salt and black pepper

1 Break the cauliflower and broccoli
into florets and cook in lightly
salted, boiling water for 8–10 minutes,
until just tender. Drain well and transfer to a flameproof dish.

2 Mix together the yogurt, shredded
cheese, and mustard, then season
the mixture with pepper and spoon
over the cauliflower and broccoli.

3 Sprinkle the bread crumbs over the
top and place under a broiler until
golden brown. Serve hot.

COOK'S TIP
When preparing the cauliflower
and broccoli, discard the tougher
part of the stalk, then break the
florets into even-sized pieces, so
they cook evenly.

NUTRITION NOTES

Per portion:

Energy	144Kcals/601kJ
Fat	6.5g
Saturated fat	3.25g
Cholesterol	16.5mg
Fiber	3.25g

WATERCRESS AND POTATO SALAD

New potatoes are equally good hot or cold, and this colorful, nutritious salad is an ideal way of making the most of them.

INGREDIENTS

Serves 4

1 lb small new potatoes, unpeeled
1 bunch watercress
1½ cups cherry tomatoes, halved
2 tbsp pumpkin seeds
3 tbsp low fat fromage frais
1 tbsp cider vinegar
1 tsp brown sugar
salt and paprika

1 Cook the potatoes in lightly salted, boiling water until just tender, then drain and leave to cool.

2 Toss together the potatoes, watercress, tomatoes, and pumpkin seeds.

3 Place the fromage frais, vinegar, sugar, salt, and paprika in a screw-top jar and shake well to mix. Pour over the salad just before serving.

NUTRITION NOTES

Per portion:

Energy	150Kcals/630kJ
Fat	4.15g
Saturated fat	0.81g
Cholesterol	0.11mg
Fiber	2.55g

COOK'S TIP
If you are packing this salad for a picnic, take the dressing in the jar and toss in just before serving.

TRICOLOR SALAD

A refreshing salad that goes well with broiled meats or fish. Alternatively, arrange it prettily on individual plates and serve as a summer starter.

INGREDIENTS

Serves 4

2 medium cooked beet, diced
2 Belgian endives, sliced
1 large orange
4 tbsp plain low fat yogurt
2 tsp whole-grain mustard
salt and black pepper

1 Mix together the diced, cooked beet and sliced Belgian endive in a large serving bowl.

2 Finely grate the rind from the orange. With a sharp knife, remove all the peel and white pith. Cut out the segments, catching the juice in a bowl. Add the segments to the salad.

3 Add the orange rind, yogurt, mustard, and seasonings to the orange juice, mix thoroughly, then spoon over the salad.

COOK'S TIP
Fresh baby spinach leaves or rocket could be used in place of the Belgian endive, if you prefer.

NUTRITION NOTES

Per portion:

Energy	41Kcals/172kJ
Fat	0.6g
Saturated fat	0.08g
Cholesterol	0.6mg
Fiber	1.42g

ROASTED BELL PEPPER SALAD

This colorful salad is very easy and can be made up to a day in advance, as the sharp-sweet dressing mingles with the mild pepper flavors.

INGREDIENTS

Serves 4

3 large red, green and yellow bell
  peppers, halved and seeded
4oz feta cheese, diced or crumbled
1 tbsp sherry vinegar or red wine
  vinegar
1 tbsp clear honey
salt and black pepper

1 Arrange the bell pepper halves in a single layer, skin side up, on a baking sheet. Place the bell peppers under a hot broiler until the skin is blackened and beginning to blister.

2 Lift the peppers into a plastic bag and close the end. Leave until cool, then peel off and discard the skin.

3 Arrange the bell peppers on a platter and scatter over the cheese. Mix together the vinegar, honey, and seasonings, then sprinkle over the salad. Chill until ready to serve.

NUTRITION NOTES

Per portion:

Energy	110Kcals/462kJ
Fat	6.15g
Saturated fat	3.65g
Cholesterol	20.13mg
Fiber	1.84g

ROSEMARY ROASTIES

These unusual roast potatoes use far less fat than traditional roast potatoes, and because they still have their skins they not only absorb less oil but have more flavor too.

───── INGREDIENTS ─────

Serves 4
2 lb small red potatoes
2 tsp walnut or sunflower oil
2 tbsp fresh rosemary leaves
salt and paprika

1 Preheat the oven to 475°F. Leave the potatoes whole with the peel on, or if large, cut in half. Place the potatoes in a large pan of cold water and bring to a boil. Drain well.

2 Drizzle the walnut or sunflower oil over the potatoes and shake the pan to coat them evenly.

3 Tip the potatoes into a shallow roasting pan. Sprinkle with rosemary, salt, and paprika. Roast for 30 minutes or until crisp. Serve hot.

───── **NUTRITION NOTES** ─────

Per portion:
Energy	205Kcals/865kJ
Fat	2.22g
Saturated fat	0.19g
Cholesterol	0
Fiber	3.25g

BAKED ZUCCHINI IN TOMATO SAUCE

───── INGREDIENTS ─────

Serves 4
1 tsp olive oil
3 large zucchini, thinly sliced
½ small red onion, finely chopped
1¼ cups tomato sauce
2 tbsp chopped fresh thyme
garlic salt and black pepper
fresh thyme sprigs, to garnish

1 Preheat the oven to 375°F. Brush an ovenproof dish with olive oil. Arrange half the zucchini and onion in the dish.

2 Spoon half the tomato sauce over the vegetables and sprinkle with some of the fresh thyme, then season to taste with garlic salt and pepper.

3 Arrange the remaining zucchini and onion in the dish on top of the sauce, then season to taste with more garlic salt and pepper. Spoon over the remaining sauce and spread evenly.

4 Cover the dish with foil, then bake for 40–45 minutes, or until the zucchini is tender. Garnish with sprigs of thyme and serve hot.

───── **NUTRITION NOTES** ─────

Per portion:
Energy	49Kcals/205kJ
Fat	1.43g
Saturated fat	0.22g
Cholesterol	0
Fiber	1.73g

Hot Desserts

Dessert lovers will be glad to learn that desserts need not be taboo for low fat diets. There are lots of ways to cook quite substantial desserts without the need for rich, high-fat mixtures. Classic crisps can be made a little less sinful and far more exciting by adding less fat and more crunch in the form of oatmeal or nuts. Skim or semi-skim milk, with a little whisked egg white, will lighten a milk pudding, and egg whites can be used in place of whole eggs for pancakes or cakes. For a change, try an unusual couscous or bread crumb mixture instead of a heavy sponge pudding. Even a delicious, sticky Gingerbread Upside Down Cake can be made with just a little oil and the minimum of eggs, with no loss of appeal.

Banana Maple, and Lime Crêpes

Crêpes are a treat any day of the week, and they can be made in advance and stored in the freezer for convenience.

Ingredients

Serves 4
1 cup flour
1 egg white
1 cup skim milk
¼ cup cold water
sunflower oil, for frying

For the filling
4 bananas, sliced
3 tbsp maple syrup
2 tbsp lime juice
strips of lime rind, to decorate

1 Beat together the flour, egg white, milk, and water until smooth and bubbly. Chill until needed.

2 Heat a small amount of oil in a nonstick frying pan and pour in enough batter just to coat the base. Swirl it around the pan to coat evenly.

3 Cook until golden, then toss or turn and cook the other side. Place on a plate, cover with foil, and keep hot while making the remaining crêpes.

4 To make the filling, place the bananas, syrup, and lime juice in a pan and simmer gently for 1 minute. Spoon into the crêpes and fold into quarters. Sprinkle with shreds of lime rind to decorate. Serve hot, with yogurt or low fat fromage frais.

Cook's Tip
Crêpes freeze well. To store for later use, interleave them with nonstick baking paper, wrap, and freeze for up to 3 months.

NUTRITION NOTES

Per portion:

Energy	282Kcals/1185kJ
Fat	2.79g
Saturated fat	0.47g
Cholesterol	1.25mg
Fiber	2.12g

SPICED PEARS IN CIDER

Any variety of pear can be used for cooking, but it is best to choose firm pears for this recipe, or they will break up easily – Bosc are a good choice.

INGREDIENTS

Serves 4

4 medium firm pears
1 cup dry cider
thinly pared strip of lemon rind
1 cinnamon stick
2 tbsp brown sugar
1 tsp arrowroot
ground cinnamon, to sprinkle

1 Peel the pears thinly, leaving them whole with the stems on. Place in a pan with the cider, lemon rind, and cinnamon. Cover and simmer gently, turning the pears occasionally for 15–20 minutes, or until tender.

2 Lift out the pears. Boil the syrup, uncovered, to reduce by about half. Remove the lemon rind and cinnamon stick, then stir in the sugar.

3 Mix the arrowroot with 1 tbsp cold water in a small bowl until smooth, then stir into the syrup. Bring to a boil and stir over the heat until thickened and clear.

4 Pour the sauce over the pears and sprinkle with ground cinnamon. Leave to cool slightly, then serve warm with low fat fromage frais.

COOK'S TIP
Whole pears look very impressive, but if you prefer, they can be halved and cored before cooking. This will reduce the cooking time slightly.

NUTRITION NOTES

Per portion:

Energy	102Kcals/428kJ
Fat	0.18g
Saturated fat	0.01g
Cholesterol	0
Fiber	1.65g

SNOW-CAPPED APPLES

INGREDIENTS

Serves 4

4 tart baking apples
6 tbsp orange marmalade or jam
2 egg whites
4 tbsp sugar

1 Preheat the oven to 350°F. Core the apples and score through the skins around the middle with a sharp knife.

2 Place in a wide ovenproof dish and spoon 1 tbsp marmalade into the center of each. Cover and bake for 35–40 minutes, or until tender.

3 Whisk the egg whites in a large bowl until stiff enough to hold soft peaks. Whisk in the sugar, then fold in the remaining marmalade.

4 Spoon the meringue over the apples, then return to the oven for 10–15 minutes, or until golden. Serve hot.

NUTRITION NOTES

Per portion:

Energy	165Kcals/394kJ
Fat	0.16g
Saturated fat	0
Cholesterol	0
Fiber	1.9g

STRAWBERRY AND APPLE TART

INGREDIENTS

Serves 4–6

1¼ cups self-rising flour
⅔ cup oatmeal
4 tbsp sunflower margarine
2 tart baking apples, about 1 lb total weight
2 cups strawberries, halved
4 tbsp sugar
1 tbsp cornstarch

1 Preheat the oven to 400°F. Mix together the flour and oatmeal in a large bowl and rub in the margarine evenly. Stir in just enough cold water to bind the mixture to a firm dough. Knead lightly until smooth.

2 Roll out the pastry and line a 9in loose-based tart pan. Trim the edges, prick the base, and line with baking paper and baking beans. Roll out the pastry trimmings and stamp out heart shapes using a cutter.

3 Bake the pastry shell for 10 minutes, remove paper and beans, and bake for 10–15 minutes or until golden brown. Bake the hearts until golden.

4 Peel, core, and slice the apples. Place in a pan with the strawberries, sugar, and cornstarch. Cover and cook gently, stirring, until the fruit is just tender. Spoon into the pastry shell and decorate with pastry hearts.

NUTRITION NOTES

Per portion:

Energy	382Kcals/1602kJ
Fat	11.93g
Saturated fat	2.18g
Cholesterol	0.88mg
Fiber	4.37g

FRUITY BREAD PUDDING

A delicious family favorite from grandmother's day, with a lighter, healthier touch.

— INGREDIENTS —

Serves 4

⅔ cup mixed dried fruit
⅔ cup apple juice
1¼ cups stale whole-wheat or white
    bread, diced
1 tsp cinnamon
1 large banana, sliced
⅔ cup skim milk
1 tbsp raw sugar
plain low fat yogurt, to serve

1 Preheat the oven to 400°F. Place the dried fruit in a small pan with the apple juice and bring to a boil.

2 Remove the pan from the heat and stir in the bread, spice, and banana. Spoon the mixture into a shallow 5 cup ovenproof dish and pour over the milk.

3 Sprinkle with raw sugar and bake for 25–30 minutes, until firm and golden brown. Serve hot or cold with plain yogurt.

COOK'S TIP
Different types of bread will absorb varying amounts of liquid, so you may need to adjust the amount of milk to allow for this.

— NUTRITION NOTES —

Per portion:

Energy	190Kcals/800kJ
Fat	0.89g
Saturated fat	0.21g
Cholesterol	0.75mg
Fiber	1.8g

SOUFFLÉED ORANGE SEMOLINA

Semolina has a reputation as a rather dull, sloppy pudding, but cooked like this you would hardly recognize it.

INGREDIENTS

Serves 4
¼ cup semolina flour
2½ cups low fat milk
2 tbsp brown sugar
1 large orange
1 egg white

1 Preheat the oven to 400°F. Place the semolina in a nonstick pan with the milk and sugar. Stir over a moderate heat until thickened and smooth. Remove from the heat.

2 Grate a few long shreds of orange rind from the orange and save for decoration. Finely grate the remaining rind. Cut all the peel and white pith from the orange and remove the segments. Stir into the semolina with the orange rind.

3 Whisk the egg white until stiff but not dry, then fold lightly and evenly into the mixture. Spoon into a 4 cup ovenproof dish and bake for 15–20 minutes, until puffed and golden brown. Serve immediately.

COOK'S TIP
When using the rind of citrus fruit, scrub the fruit thoroughly before use, or buy unwaxed fruit.

NUTRITION NOTES

Per portion:
Energy	158Kcals/665kJ
Fat	2.67g
Saturated fat	1.54g
Cholesterol	10.5mg
Fiber	0.86g

SPICED RED FRUIT COMPOTE

INGREDIENTS

Serves 4

4 ripe red plums, halved
2 cups strawberries, halved
1¾ cups raspberries
2 tbsp brown sugar
2 tbsp cold water
1 cinnamon stick
3 pieces star anise
6 cloves

NUTRITION NOTES

Per portion:

Energy	90Kcals/375kJ
Fat	0.32g
Saturated fat	0
Cholesterol	0
Fiber	3.38g

1 Place the plums, strawberries, and raspberies in a heavy-based pan with the sugar and water.

2 Add the cinnamon stick, star anise, and cloves to the pan and heat gently, without boiling, until the sugar dissolves and the fruit juices run.

3 Cover the pan and leave the fruit to infuse over very low heat for about 5 minutes. Remove the spices from the compote before serving warm, with plain yogurt or fromage frais.

RHUBARB SPIRAL COBBLER

INGREDIENTS

Serves 4

1½ lb rhubarb, sliced
4 tbsp granulated sugar
3 tbsp orange juice
1⅓ cups self-rising flour
2 tbsp superfine sugar
about 1 cup plain yogurt
grated rind of 1 medium orange
2 tbsp raw sugar
1 tsp ground ginger

1 Preheat the oven to 400°F. Cook the rhubarb, sugar, and orange juice in a covered pan until tender. Tip into an ovenproof dish.

2 To make the topping, mix the flour, superfine sugar, and enough yogurt to bind to a soft dough.

3 Roll out on a floured surface to a 10in square. Mix the orange rind, raw sugar, and ginger, then sprinkle this over the dough.

4 Roll up quite tightly, then cut into about 10 slices using a sharp knife. Arrange the slices over the rhubarb.

5 Bake in the oven for 15–20 minutes, or until the spirals are puffed and golden brown. Serve warm, with ordinary or frozen yogurt.

NUTRITION NOTES

Per portion:

Energy	320Kcals/1343kJ
Fat	1.2g
Saturated fat	0.34g
Cholesterol	2mg
Fiber	3.92g

CRUNCHY GOOSEBERRY CRISP

Gooseberries are perfect for traditional family desserts like this one. When they are out of season, other fruits such as apple, plums, or rhubarb could be used instead.

INGREDIENTS

Serves 4

5 cups gooseberries
4 tbsp granulated sugar
1 cup oatmeal
¾ cup whole-wheat flour
4 tbsp sunflower oil
4 tbsp raw sugar
2 tbsp chopped walnuts
plain yogurt, to serve

1 Preheat the oven to 400°F. Place the gooseberries in a pan with the granulated sugar. Cover and cook over low heat for 10 minutes, until the gooseberries are just tender. Tip into an oven-proof dish.

2 To make the crisp, place the oatmeal, flour, and oil in a bowl and stir with a fork until evenly mixed.

3 Stir in the raw sugar and walnuts, then spread evenly over the gooseberries. Bake for 25–30 minutes, or until golden and bubbling. Serve hot with yogurt.

COOK'S TIP
The best cooking gooseberries are the early small, firm green ones.

NUTRITION NOTES

Per portion:

Energy	422Kcals/1770kJ
Fat	18.5g
Saturated fat	2.32g
Cholesterol	0
Fiber	5.12g

GINGERBREAD UPSIDE-DOWN CAKE

The perfect warmer-upper on a cold winter's day. This one is quite quick to make and looks very impressive.

INGREDIENTS

Serves 4–6

sunflower oil, for brushing
1 tbsp brown sugar
4 medium peaches, halved and pitted, or canned peach halves
8 walnut halves

For the base
½ cup whole-wheat flour
½ tsp baking soda
1½ tsp ground ginger
1 tsp ground cinnamon
½ cup brown sugar
1 egg
½ cup skim milk
¼ cup sunflower oil

1 Preheat the oven to 350°F. For the topping, brush the base and sides of a 9in round spring form cake pan with oil. Sprinkle the sugar over the base.

2 Arrange the peaches cut-side down in the pan with a walnut half in each.

3 For the base, sift together the flour, baking soda, ginger, and cinnamon, then stir in the sugar. Beat together the egg, milk and oil, then mix into the dry ingredients until smooth.

4 Pour the mixture evenly over the peaches and bake for 35–40 minutes, until firm to the touch. Turn out onto a serving plate. Serve hot with yogurt or low fat ice cream.

NUTRITION NOTES

Per portion:	
Energy	432Kcals/1812kJ
Fat	16.54g
Saturated fat	2.27g
Cholesterol	48.72mg
Fiber	4.79g

HOT PLUM BATTER

Other fruits can be used in place of plums, depending on the season. Canned black cherries are also a convenient pantry substitute.

──── INGREDIENTS ────

Serves 4

1 lb ripe red plums, quartered and
*   pitted*
⅞ cup skim milk
4 tbsp skim milk powder
1 tbsp brown sugar
1 tsp vanilla extract
3oz self-rising flour
2 egg whites
confectioners' sugar, to sprinkle

1 Preheat the oven to 425°F. Lightly oil a wide, shallow ovenproof dish and add the plums.

2 Pour the milk, milk powder, sugar, vanilla, flour, and egg whites into a food processor. Process until smooth.

3 Pour the batter over the plums. Bake for 25–30 minutes, or until puffed and golden. Sprinkle with confectioners' sugar and serve hot.

──── NUTRITION NOTES ────

Per portion:

Energy	195Kcals/816kJ
Fat	0.48g
Saturated fat	0.12g
Cholesterol	2.8mg
Fiber	2.27g

GLAZED APRICOT PUDDING

British-style puddings are usually very high in saturated fat, but this one uses the minimum of oil and no eggs.

──── INGREDIENTS ────

Serves 4

2 tsp golden syrup
14oz can apricot halves in fruit juice
1¼ cup self-rising flour
1½ cups fresh bread crumbs
⅔ cup brown sugar
1 tsp ground cinnamon
2 tbsp sunflower oil
¾ cup skim milk

1 Preheat the oven to 350°F. Lightly oil a cup pudding bowl. Spoon in the syrup.

2 Drain the apricots and reserve the juice. Arrange about 8 halves in the basin. Purée the rest of the apricots with the juice and set aside.

3 Mix the flour, bread crumbs, sugar, and cinnamon, then beat in the oil and milk. Spoon into the bowl and bake for 50–55 minutes, or until firm and golden. Turn out and serve with the puréed fruit as a sauce.

──── NUTRITION NOTES ────

Per portion:

Energy	364Kcals/1530kJ
Fat	6.47g
Saturated fat	0.89g
Cholesterol	0.88mg
Fiber	2.37g

PLUM FILA POCKETS

INGREDIENTS

Serves 4

½ *cup low fat cream cheese*
1 tbsp brown sugar
½ *tsp ground cloves*
8 large, firm plums, halved and pitted
8 sheets fila pastry
sunflower oil, for brushing
confectioners' sugar, to sprinkle

1 Preheat the oven to 425°F. Mix together the low fat cream cheese, sugar, and cloves.

2 Sandwich the plum halves back together in pairs with a spoonful of the cheese mixture.

3 Spread out the pastry and cut into 16 pieces, about 9in square. Brush one lightly with oil and place a second at a diagonal on top. Repeat with the remaining squares.

4 Place a plum on each pastry square, and pinch corners together. Place on baking sheet. Bake for 15–18 minutes, until golden, then dust with sugar.

NUTRITION NOTES

Per portion:
Energy	188Kcals/790kJ
Fat	1.87g
Saturated fat	0.27g
Cholesterol	0.29mg
Fiber	2.55g

APPLE-COUSCOUS PUDDING

This unusual mixture makes a delicious family dessert with a rich fruity flavor, but virtually no fat.

INGREDIENTS

Serves 4

2½ *cups apple juice*
⅔ *cup couscous*
¼ *cup raisins*
½ *tsp mixed spice*
1 large tart baking apple, peeled, cored, and sliced
2 tbsp raw sugar
plain low fat yogurt, to serve

1 Preheat the oven to 400°F. Place the apple juice, couscous, raisins, and spice in a pan and bring to a boil, stirring. Cover and simmer for 10–12 minutes, until all the liquid is absorbed.

2 Spoon half the couscous mixture into a 5 cup ovenproof dish and top with half the apple slices. Top with remaining couscous.

3 Arrange the remaining apple slices overlapping over the top and sprinkle with raw sugar. Bake for 25–30 minutes, or until golden brown. Serve hot, with yogurt.

NUTRITION NOTES

Per portion:
Energy	194Kcals/815kJ
Fat	0.58g
Saturated fat	0.09g
Cholesterol	0
Fiber	0.75g

COLD DESSERTS

From fresh, colorful fruit salads to refreshing, tangy sorbets, healthy cold desserts should be the easiest part of selecting dishes for your low fat menus. The year-round huge variety of fresh fruit gives a head start – even the simplest platter of fresh fruits can make an exotic dessert. Time was when ice creams, mousses, and cheesecakes were without exception rich, elaborate and high in fat, certainly to be avoided in excess. But the rapidly expanding range of low fat dairy products such as fromage frais, yogurt, and crème fraîche, means that lighter, far less rich versions are now possible. So, if plain fresh fruit is just not enough, you can tuck into a luscious scoop of Banana Honey Yogurt Ice or a slice of Creamy Mango Cheesecake without a trace of guilt.

FRUITED RICE RING

This unusual rice pudding looks beautiful turned out of a ring mold but if you prefer, stir the fruit into the rice and serve in individual dishes.

INGREDIENTS

Serves 4
5 tbsp short-grain rice
3¾ cups low fat milk
1 cinnamon stick
1½ cups mixed dried fruit
¾ cup orange juice
3 tbsp sugar
finely grated rind of 1 small orange

1 Place the rice, milk, and cinnamon stick in a large pan and bring to a boil. Cover and simmer, stirring occasionally, for about 1½ hours, until no liquid remains.

2 Meanwhile, place the fruit and orange juice in another pan and bring to a boil. Cover and simmer very gently for about 1 hour, until tender and no liquid remains.

3 Remove the cinnamon stick from the rice and stir in the sugar and orange rind.

4 Tip the fruit into the base of a lightly oiled 6 cup ring mold. Spoon the rice over, smoothing down firmly. Chill.

5 Run a knife around the edge of the mold and turn out the rice carefully on to a serving plate.

NUTRITION NOTES	
Per portion:	
Energy	343Kcals/1440kJ
Fat	4.4g
Saturated fat	2.26g
Cholesterol	15.75mg
Fiber	1.07g

RASPBERRY-PASSIONFRUIT SWIRLS

If passionfruit is not available, this simple dessert can be made with raspberries alone.

INGREDIENTS

Serves 4
2½ cups raspberries
2 passionfruit
1⅔ cups low fat fromage frais
2 tbsp sugar
raspberries and sprigs of mint, to
  decorate

1 Mash the raspberries in a small bowl with a fork until the juice runs. Scoop out the passionfruit pulp into a separate bowl with the fromage frais and sugar and mix well.

2 Spoon alternate spoonfuls of the raspberry pulp and the fromage frais mixture into stemmed glasses or one large serving dish, stirring lightly to create a swirled effect.

3 Decorate each dessert with a whole raspberry and a sprig of fresh mint. Serve chilled.

COOK'S TIP
Over-ripe, slightly soft fruit can also be used in this recipe. Use frozen raspberries when fresh are not available, but thaw first.

NUTRITION NOTES

Per portion:
Energy	110Kcals/462kJ
Fat	0.47g
Saturated fat	0.13g
Cholesterol	1mg
Fiber	2.12g

CREAMY MANGO CHEESECAKE

Cheesecakes are always a favorite but sadly they are often high in fat. This one is the exception.

INGREDIENTS

Serves 4

1¼ cups oatmeal
3 tbsp sunflower margarine
2 tbsp clear honey
1 large ripe mango
1¼ cups low fat cream cheese
⅔ cup low fat plain yogurt
finely grated rind of 1 small lime
3 tbsp apple juice
4 tsp powdered gelatin
fresh mango and lime slices, to decorate

1 Preheat the oven to 400°F. Mix together the oatmeal, margarine, and honey. Press the mixture into the base of a 8in loose-bottomed cake pan. Bake for 12–15 minutes, until lightly browned. Cool.

2 Peel, pit, and roughly chop the mango. Place the chopped mango, cheese, yogurt, and lime rind in a food processor and process until smooth.

3 Heat the apple juice until boiling, sprinkle the gelatin over it, stir to dissolve, then stir into cheese mixture.

4 Pour the cheese mixture into the pan and chill until set, then turn out onto a serving plate. Decorate the top with mango and lime slices.

NUTRITION NOTES

Per portion:

Energy	422Kcals/1774kJ
Fat	11.37g
Saturated fat	2.2g
Cholesterol	2.95mg
Fiber	7.15g

FRUDITÉS WITH HONEY DIP

INGREDIENTS

Serves 4

1 cup thick, plain, yogurt
3 tbsp clear honey
selection of fresh fruit for dipping such as apples, pears, tangerines, grapes, figs, cherries, strawberries, and kiwi fruit

NUTRITION NOTES

Per portion:

Energy	161Kcals/678kJ
Fat	5.43g
Saturated fat	3.21g
Cholesterol	7.31mg
Fiber	2.48g

1 Place the yogurt in a dish, beat until smooth, then stir in the honey, leaving a little marbled effect.

2 Cut the fruits into wedges or bite-sized pieces, or leave whole.

3 Arrange the fruits on a platter with the bowl of dip in the center. Serve chilled.

APRICOT MOUSSE

This light, fluffy dessert can be made with any dried fruits instead of apricots – try dried peaches, prunes, or apples.

INGREDIENTS

Serves 4

1½ cups dried apricots
1¼ cups fresh orange juice
⅞ cup low fat fromage frais
2 egg whites
mint sprigs, to decorate

1 Place the apricots in a saucepan with the orange juice and heat gently until boiling. Cover the pan and simmer gently for 3 minutes.

2 Cool slightly. Place in a food processor or blender and process until smooth. Stir in the fromage frais.

3 Whisk the egg whites until stiff enough to hold soft peaks, then fold into the apricot mixture.

4 Spoon into four stemmed glasses or one large serving dish. Chill before serving.

COOK'S TIP
For an even quicker version, omit the egg whites and simply swirl together the apricot mixture and fromage frais.

NUTRITION NOTES

Per portion:

Energy	180Kcals/757kJ
Fat	0.63g
Saturated fat	0.06g
Cholesterol	0.5mg
Fiber	4.8g

APPLE FOAM WITH BLACKBERRIES

Any seasonal berry can be used for this if blackberries are not available.

INGREDIENTS

Serves 4
2 cups blackberries
⅔ cup apple juice
1 tsp powdered gelatin
1 tbsp clear honey
2 egg whites

1 Place the blackberries in a pan with 4 tbsp of the apple juice and heat gently until the fruit is soft. Remove from the heat, cool, and chill.

2 Sprinkle the gelatin over the remaining apple juice in a small pan and stir over low heat until dissolved. Stir in the honey.

3 Whisk the egg whites until they hold stiff peaks. Continue whisking hard and pour in the hot gelatin mixture gradually, until well mixed.

4 Quickly spoon the foam into rough mounds on individual plates. Chill. Serve with the blackberries and juice spooned around.

COOK'S TIP
Make sure that you dissolve the gelatin over very low heat. It must not boil, or it will lose its setting ability.

NUTRITION NOTES

Per portion:

Energy	49Kcals/206kJ
Fat	0.15g
Saturated fat	0
Cholesterol	0
Fiber	1.74g

GRAPE CHEESE WHIP

INGREDIENTS

Serves 4

1 cup purple or green seedless grapes,
* plus 4 sprigs*
2 egg whites
1 tbsp sugar
finely grated rind and juice of ½ lemon
1 cup low fat cream cheese
3 tbsp clear honey
2 tbsp brandy (optional)

NUTRITION NOTES

Per portion:

Energy	135Kcals/563kJ
Fat	0
Saturated fat	0
Cholesterol	0.56mg
Fiber	0

1 Brush the sprigs of grapes lightly with egg white and sprinkle with sugar to coat. Leave to dry.

2 Mix together the lemon rind and juice, cheese, honey, and brandy. Chop the remaining grapes and stir in.

3 Whisk the egg whites until stiff enough to hold soft peaks. Fold the whites into the grape mixture, then spoon into serving glasses.

4 Top with sugar-frosted grapes and serve chilled.

STRAWBERRIES IN SPICED GRAPE JELLY

INGREDIENTS

Serves 4

1⅞ cups red grape juice
1 cinnamon stick
1 small orange
1 envelope gelatin
2 cups strawberries, chopped
strawberries and orange rind, to
* decorate*

1 Place the grape juice in a pan with the cinnamon. Thinly pare the rind from the orange and add to the pan. Infuse over a very low heat for 10 minutes, then remove the flavorings.

2 Squeeze the juice from the orange and sprinkle over the gelatin. Stir into the grape juice to dissolve. Allow to cool until just beginning to set.

3 Stir in the strawberries and quickly tip into a 4 cup mold or serving dish. Chill until set.

4 To turn out, dip the mold quickly into hot water and invert onto a serving plate. Decorate with fresh strawberries and shreds of orange rind.

NUTRITION NOTES

Per portion:

Energy	85Kcals/355kJ
Fat	0.2g
Saturated fat	0
Cholesterol	0
Fiber	1.04g

PLUM AND PORT SORBET

This is more of a sorbet for grown-ups, but you could use red grape juice in place of the port if you prefer.

INGREDIENTS

Serves 4–6
2 lb ripe red plums, halved and pitted
6 tbsp sugar
3 tbsp water
3 tbsp ruby port or red wine
plain cookies, to serve

1 Place the plums in a pan with the sugar and water. Stir over gentle heat until the sugar is melted, then cover and simmer gently for about 5 minutes, until the fruit is soft.

2 Turn into a food processor and purée until smooth, then stir in the port. Cool completely, then tip into a freezer container and freeze until firm around the edges.

3 Spoon into the food processor and process until smooth. Return to the freezer and freeze until solid.

4 Allow to soften slightly at room temperature for 15–20 minutes before serving in scoops, with plain cookies.

NUTRITION NOTES

Per portion:
Energy	166Kcals/699kJ
Fat	0.25g
Saturated fat	0
Cholesterol	0
Fiber	3.75g

TOFU BERRY BRULÉE

This is a lighter variation of a classic dessert, usually forbidden on a low fat diet, using tofu, which is low in fat and free from cholesterol. Use any soft berry fruits in season.

INGREDIENTS

Serves 4

11oz packet tofu
3 tbsp confectioners' sugar
1½ cups red berries, such as raspberries,
  strawberries, and red currants
about 5 tbsp raw sugar

1 Place the tofu and confectioners' sugar in a food processor or blender and process until smooth.

2 Stir in the fruits and spoon into a 3¾ cup flameproof dish. Sprinkle the top with enough raw sugar to cover evenly.

3 Place under a very hot broiler until the sugar melts and caramelizes. Chill before serving.

COOK'S TIP
Choose smooth tofu rather than firm tofu as it gives a better texture in this type of dish. Firm tofu is better for cooking in chunks.

NUTRITION NOTES

Per portion:	
Energy	180Kcals/760kJ
Fat	3.01g
Saturated fat	0.41g
Cholesterol	0
Fiber	1.31g

EMERALD FRUIT SALAD

INGREDIENTS

Serves 4

2 tbsp lime juice
2 tbsp clear honey
2 green eating apples, cored and sliced
1 small ripe melon, diced
2 kiwi fruit, sliced
1 star fruit, sliced
mint sprigs, to decorate

1 Mix together the lime juice and honey in a large bowl, then toss the apple slices in this.

2 Stir in the melon, kiwi fruit and star fruit. Place in a glass serving dish and chill before serving.

3 Decorate with mint sprigs and serve with yogurt or fromage frais.

COOK'S TIP
Star fruit is best when fully ripe – look for plump, yellow fruit.

NUTRITION NOTES

Per portion:

Energy	93Kcals/390kJ
Fat	0.48g
Saturated fat	0
Cholesterol	0
Fiber	2.86g

PEACH AND GINGER PASHKA

This simpler adaptation of a Russian Easter favorite is made with much lighter ingredients than the traditional version.

INGREDIENTS

Serves 4–6

1½ cups low fat cottage cheese
2 ripe peaches or nectarines
⅓ cup low fat plain yogurt
2 pieces preserved ginger in syrup, drained and chopped
2 tbsp ginger syrup
½ tsp vanilla extract
peach slices and toasted slivered almonds, to decorate

NUTRITION NOTES

Per portion:

Energy	142Kcals/600kJ
Fat	1.63g
Saturated fat	0.22g
Cholesterol	1.77mg
Fiber	1.06g

1 Drain the cottage cheese and press through a strainer into a bowl. Pit and roughly chop the peaches.

2 Mix together the chopped peaches, cottage cheese, yogurt, ginger, syrup, and vanilla extract.

3 Line a new, clean flower pot or a strainer with a piece of clean, fine cloth such as cheesecloth.

4 Tip in the cheese mixture, then wrap over the cloth and place a weight on top. Leave over a bowl in a cool place to drain overnight. To serve, unwrap the cloth and invert the pashka on to a plate. Decorate with peach slices and almonds.

BANANA-HONEY YOGURT ICE

INGREDIENTS

Serves 4–6

4 ripe bananas, chopped coarsely
1 tbsp lemon juice
2 tbsp clear honey
1 cup thick, plain yogurt
½ tsp ground cinnamon
plain cookies, slivered hazelnuts, and
banana slices, to serve

NUTRITION NOTES

Per portion:
Energy	138Kcals/580kJ
Fat	7.37g
Saturated fat	3.72g
Cholesterol	8.13mg
Fiber	0.47g

1 Place the bananas in a food processor or blender with the lemon juice, honey, yogurt, and cinnamon. Process until smooth and creamy.

2 Pour the mixture into a freezer container and freeze until almost solid. Spoon back into the food processor and process again until smooth.

3 Return to the freezer until firm. Allow to soften at room temperature for 15 minutes, then serve in scoops, with plain cookies, slivered hazelnuts, and banana slices.

AUTUMN PUDDING

INGREDIENTS

Serves 6

10 slices white or whole-wheat bread,
at least 1 day old
1 tart cooking apple, peeled, cored, and
sliced
8oz ripe red plums, halved and pitted
8oz blackberries
4 tbsp water
6 tbsp sugar

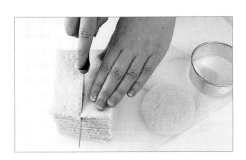

1 Remove the crusts from the bread and use a cookie cutter to stamp out a 3in round from one slice. Cut the remaining slices in half.

2 Place the bread round in the base of a 5 cup pudding bowl, then overlap the fingers around the sides, saving some for the top.

3 Place the apple, plums, blackberries, water, and sugar in a pan, heat gently until the sugar dissolves, then simmer gently for 10 minutes, or until soft. Remove from the heat.

4 Reserve the juice and spoon the fruit into the bread-lined bowl. Top with the reserved bread, then spoon over the reserved fruit juices.

5 Cover the mold with a saucer and place weights on top. Chill the pudding overnight. Turn out onto a serving plate and serve with low fat yogurt or fromage frais.

NUTRITION NOTES

Per portion:
Energy	197Kcals/830kJ
Fat	1.1g
Saturated fat	0.2g
Cholesterol	0
Fiber	2.84g

CAKES AND BAKES

The main advantage of baking your own cakes and cookies is that you can control exactly what goes into them. Most commercially produced cakes and bakes contain a high proportion of saturated fats, but it is possible to bake at home using less fat, different types of fat, and often less sugar too. All the bakes in this chapter are low in fat, and in many cases contain little or no eggs, and often sugar is reduced by using fruits to sweeten the mixture. The main drawback is that the cakes will not keep for nearly as long as traditional recipes, but it is a problem far outweighed by the health advantages. So, as you fill the cookie jar with Apricot Yogurt Cookies or serve up that luscious slice of Carrot Cake, your conscience is clear – let them eat cake!

EGGLESS CHRISTMAS CAKE

Makes one 7in square cake
⅔ cup golden raisins
⅔ cup raisins
½ cup currants
⅓ cup candied cherries, halved
¼ cup cut candied peel
1 cup apple juice
¼ cup toasted hazelnuts
2 tbsp pumpkin seeds
2 pieces preserved ginger in syrup,
  chopped
finely grated rind of 1 lemon
½ cup skim milk
¼ cup sunflower oil
1¾ cups whole-wheat self-rising flour
2 tsp cinnamon
3 tbsp brandy or dark rum
apricot jam, for brushing
candied fruits, to decorate

1 Place the golden raisins, raisins, currants, cherries, and peel in a bowl and stir in the apple juice. Cover and leave to soak overnight.

2 Preheat the oven to 300°F. Grease and line a 7in square cake pan.

3 Add the hazelnuts, pumpkin seeds, ginger, and lemon rind to the soaked fruit. Stir in the milk and oil. Sift together the flour and spice, and stir into the mixture with the brandy or rum.

4 Spoon into the prepared pan and bake for about 1½ hours, or until the cake is golden brown and firm to the touch.

5 Turn out and cool on a wire rack. Brush with strained apricot jam and decorate with candied fruits.

NUTRITION NOTES

Per cake:
Energy	2702Kcals/11352kJ
Fat	73.61g
Saturated fat	10.69g
Cholesterol	2.4mg
Fiber	29.46g

CRANBERRY AND APPLE RING

Tangy cranberries add an unusual flavor to this low fat cake. It is best eaten very fresh.

INGREDIENTS

Makes 1 ring cake
2 cups self-rising flour
1 tsp ground cinnamon
½ cup brown sugar
1 crisp eating apple, cored and diced
⅔ cup fresh or frozen cranberries
4 tbsp sunflower oil
⅔ cup apple juice
cranberry jelly and apple slices, to
   decorate

1 Preheat the oven to 350°F. Lightly grease a 4 cup ring pan with oil.

2 Sift together the flour and ground cinnamon, then stir in the sugar.

3 Toss together the diced apple and cranberries. Stir into the dry ingredients, then add the oil and apple juice and beat well.

4 Spoon the mixture into the prepared ring pan and bake for about 35–40 minutes, or until the cake is firm to the touch. Turn out and leave to cool completely on a wire rack.

5 To serve, drizzle warmed cranberry jelly over the cake and decorate with apple slices.

COOK'S TIP
Fresh cranberries are available throughout the winter months and if you don't use them all at once, they can be frozen for up to a year.

NUTRITION NOTES

Per cake:
Energy	1616Kcals/6787kJ
Fat	47.34g
Saturated fat	6.14g
Cholesterol	0
Fiber	12.46g

CARROT CAKE WITH LEMON FROSTING

INGREDIENTS

Makes one 7in cake

1¾ cups whole-wheat self-rising flour
2 tsp ground allspice
⅔ cup brown sugar
3 medium carrots (about 1¼ cups),
   grated
⅓ cup golden raisins
5 tbsp sunflower oil
5 tbsp orange juice
5 tbsp skim milk
2 egg whites

For the frosting

¾ cup low fat cream cheese
finely grated rind of ½ lemon
2 tbsp clear honey
shreds of lemon rind, to decorate

1 Preheat the oven to 350°F. Grease a deep 7in round cake pan and line the base with nonstick baking paper.

2 Sift together the flour and spice, then stir in the sugar, carrots, and raisins. Mix the oil, orange juice, and milk, then stir into the dry ingredients. Whisk the egg whites until stiff, then fold in lightly and evenly.

3 Spoon into the pan and bake for 45–50 minutes, until firm and golden. Turn out and cool on a wire rack.

4 For the frosting, beat together the cheese, lemon rind, and honey until smooth. Spread over the top of the cooled cake, swirling with a metal spatula. Decorate the top with shreds of lemon rind.

NUTRITION NOTES

Per cake:	
Energy	2182Kcals/9167kJ
Fat	61.79g
Saturated fat	8.37g
Cholesterol	3.25mg
Fiber	26.65g

CHEWY FRUIT GRANOLA SLICE

INGREDIENTS

Makes 8 slices

½ cup dried apricots, chopped
1 eating apple, cored and grated
1¼ cups Swiss-style granola (muesli)
⅔ cup apple juice
1 tbsp margarine

1 Preheat the oven to 375°F. Place all the ingredients in a large bowl and mix well.

2 Press the mixture into a 20cm/8in round, nonstick shallow pie pan and bake for 35–40 minutes, or until lightly browned and firm.

3 Score into wedges with a knife and leave to cool in the pan.

NUTRITION NOTES

Per portion::	
Energy	112Kcals/467kJ
Fat	2.75g
Saturated fat	0.48g
Cholesterol	0.13mg
Fiber	2.09g

BANANA-ORANGE LOAF

For the best banana flavor and a really good, moist texture, make sure the bananas are very ripe for this cake.

— INGREDIENTS —

Makes 1 loaf
¾ *cup whole-wheat flour*
¾ *cup flour*
1 tsp baking powder
1 tsp ground mixed spice
3 tbsp slivered hazelnuts, toasted
2 large ripe bananas
1 egg
2 tbsp sunflower oil
2 tbsp clear honey
finely grated rind and juice 1 small
  orange
4 orange slices, halved
2 tsp confectioners' sugar

1 Preheat the oven to 350°F. Brush a 4 cup loaf pan with sunflower oil and line the base with nonstick baking paper.

2 Sift the flours with the baking powder and spice into a large bowl, adding any bran that is caught in the strainer. Stir the hazelnuts into the dry ingredients.

3 Peel and mash the bananas. Beat in the egg, oil, honey, and the orange rind and juice. Stir evenly into the dry ingredients.

4 Spoon into the prepared pan and smooth the top. Bake for 40–45 minutes, or until firm and golden brown. Turn out and cool on a wire rack to cool.

5 Sprinkle the orange slices with the confectioners' sugar and grill until golden. Use to decorate the cake.

COOK'S TIP
If you plan to keep the loaf for more than three days, omit the orange slices, brush with honey, and sprinkle with flaked hazelnuts.

— NUTRITION NOTES —

Per cake:

Energy	1741Kcals/7314kJ
Fat	60.74g
Saturated fat	7.39g
Cholesterol	192.5mg
Fiber	19.72g

APRICOT YOGURT COOKIES

These soft cookies are very quick to make and are useful for the cookie jar or for lunch boxes.

INGREDIENTS

Makes 16
1½ cups flour
1 tsp baking powder
1 tsp ground cinnamon
1 cup oatmeal
½ cup brown sugar
½ cup chopped dried apricots
1 tbsp slivered hazelnuts or almonds
⅔ cup plain yogurt
3 tbsp sunflower oil
raw sugar, to sprinkle

1 Preheat the oven to 375°F. Lightly oil a large baking sheet.

2 Sift together the flour, baking powder, and cinnamon. Stir in the oatmeal, sugar, apricots, and nuts.

3 Beat together the yogurt and oil, then stir evenly into the mixture to make a firm dough. If necessary, add a little more yogurt.

4 Use your hands to roll the mixture into about 16 small balls, place on the baking sheet and flatten with a fork.

5 Sprinkle with raw sugar. Bake for 15–20 minutes, or until firm and golden brown. Leave to cool on a wire rack.

COOK'S TIP
These cookies do not keep well, so it is best to eat them within two days, or to freeze them. Pack into plastic bags and freeze for up to four months.

NUTRITION NOTES

Per portion::
Energy	95Kcals/400kJ
Fat	2.66g
Saturated fat	0.37g
Cholesterol	0.3mg
Fiber	0.94g

GREEK HONEY AND LEMON CAKE

INGREDIENTS

Makes 16 slices
3 tbsp sunflower margarine
4 tbsp clear honey
finely grated rind and juice of 1 lemon
⅔ cup skim milk
1¼ cups flour
1½ tsp baking powder
½ tsp grated nutmeg
¼ cup semolina flour
2 egg whites
2 tsp sesame seeds

1 Preheat the oven to 400°F. Lightly oil a 7½in square deep cake pan and line the base with nonstick baking paper.

2 Place the margarine and 3 tbsp of the honey in a saucepan and heat gently until melted. Reserve 1 tbsp lemon juice, then stir in the rest with the lemon rind and milk.

3 Sift together the flour, baking powder, and nutmeg, then beat in with the semolina. Whisk the egg whites until they form soft peaks, then fold evenly into the mixture.

4 Spoon into the pan and sprinkle with sesame seeds. Bake for 25–30 minutes, until golden brown. Mix the reserved honey and lemon juice and drizzle over the cake while warm. Cool in the pan, then cut into fingers to serve.

NUTRITION NOTES

Per portion:

Energy	82Kcals/342kJ
Fat	2.62g
Saturated fat	0.46g
Cholesterol	0.36mg
Fiber	0.41g

STRAWBERRY ROULADE

INGREDIENTS

Serves 6
4 egg whites
⅔ cup sugar
¾ cup flour
2 tbsp orange juice
1 cup strawberries, chopped
¼ cup low fat fromage frais
sugar, for sprinkling
strawberries, to decorate

1 Preheat the oven to 400°F. Oil a 9 x 13in jelly roll pan and line with nonstick baking paper.

2 Place the egg whites in a large bowl and whisk until they form soft peaks. Gradually whisk in the sugar. Fold in half of the sifted flour, then fold in the rest with the orange juice.

3 Spoon the mixture into the prepared pan, spreading evenly. Bake for 15-18 minutes, or until golden brown and firm to the touch.

4 Meanwhile, spread out a sheet of nonstick baking paper and sprinkle with sugar. Turn out the cake on to this and remove the lining paper. Roll up the cake loosely from one short side, with the paper inside. Cool.

5 Unroll and remove the paper. Stir the strawberries into the fromage frais and spread over the sponge. Reroll and serve decorated with strawberries.

NUTRITION NOTES

Per portion:

Energy	154Kcals/646kJ
Fat	0.24g
Saturated fat	0.05g
Cholesterol	0.25mg
Fiber	0.6g

BANANA GINGER CAKE

This cake keeps well and really improves with keeping. Store it in a covered container for up to two months.

INGREDIENTS

Makes 1 cake
1¾ *cups flour*
2 *tsp baking soda*
2 *tsp ground ginger*
1¾ *cups oatmeal*
4 *tbsp brown sugar*
6 *tbsp sunflower margarine*
⅔ *cup golden syrup*
1 *egg, beaten*
3 *ripe bananas, mashed*
¾ *cup confectioners' sugar*
preserved ginger, to decorate

1 Preheat the oven to 325°F. Grease and line an 7 x 11in cake pan.

2 Sift together the flour, baking soda, and ginger, then stir in the oatmeal. Melt the sugar, margarine, and syrup in a saucepan, then stir into the flour mixture. Beat in the egg and mashed bananas.

3 Spoon into the pan and bake for about 1 hour, or until firm to the touch. Allow to cool in the pan, then turn out and cut into squares.

4 Sift the confectioners' sugar into a bowl and stir in just enough water to make a smooth, runny icing. Drizzle the icing over each square and top with a piece of preserved ginger, if you like.

COOK'S TIP
This is a nutritious, energy-giving cake that is a really good choice for lunch boxes as it doesn't break up too easily.

NUTRITION NOTES

Per cake:	
Energy	3320Kcals/13946kJ
Fat	83.65g
Saturated fat	16.34g
Cholesterol	197.75mg
Fiber	20.69g

SPICED DATE AND WALNUT CAKE

A classic flavor combination, which makes a very easy low fat, high-fiber cake.

INGREDIENTS

Makes 1 cake
2½ cups whole-wheat self-rising flour
2 tsp mixed spice
¾ cup chopped dates
½ cup chopped walnuts
4 tbsp sunflower oil
½ cup brown sugar
1¼ cups skim milk
walnut halves, to decorate

1 Preheat the oven to 350°F. Grease and line a 2 lb loaf pan with non-stick baking paper.

2 Sift together the flour and spice, returning any bran from the strainer. Stir in the dates and walnuts.

3 Mix the oil, sugar, and milk, then stir evenly into the dry ingredients. Spoon into the prepared pan and arrange the walnut halves on top.

4 Bake the cake in the oven for about 45–50 minutes, or until golden brown and firm. Turn out the cake, remove the baking paper and leave to cool on a wire rack.

NUTRITION NOTES

Per cake:

Energy	2654Kcals/11146kJ
Fat	92.78g
Saturated fat	11.44g
Cholesterol	6mg
Fiber	35.1g

COOK'S TIP
Pecans can be used in place of the walnuts in this cake.

CHERRY MARMALADE MUFFINS

— INGREDIENTS —

Makes 12
2 cups self-rising flour
1 tsp ground mixed spice
6 tbsp sugar
½ cup candied cherries, quartered
30ml/2 tbsp orange marmalade
⅔ cup skim milk
4 tbsp soft sunflower margarine
marmalade, to brush

1 Preheat the oven to 400°F. Lightly grease 12 deep muffin pans with oil.

2 Sift together the flour and spice, then stir in the sugar and cherries.

3 Mix the marmalade with the milk and beat into the dry ingredients with the margarine. Spoon into the greased pans. Bake for 20–25 minutes, until golden brown and firm.

4 Turn out on to a wire rack and brush the tops with warmed marmalade. Serve warm or cold.

— NUTRITION NOTES —

Per portion:
Energy	154Kcals/650kJ
Fat	3.66g
Saturated fat	0.68g
Cholesterol	0.54mg
Fiber	0.69g

DRIED FRUIT CAKE

— INGREDIENTS —

Makes 1 cake
¾ cup coarsely chopped mixed dried
fruit, such as apples, apricots, prunes,
and peaches
1 cup hot tea
2 cups whole-wheat self-rising flour
1 tsp grated nutmeg
4 tbsp brown sugar
3 tbsp sunflower oil
3 tbsp skim milk
raw sugar, to sprinkle

— NUTRITION NOTES —

Per cake:
Energy	1615Kcals/6786kJ
Fat	39.93g
Saturated fat	5.22g
Cholesterol	0.9mg
Fiber	31.12g

1 Soak the dried fruits in the tea for several hours or overnight. Drain and reserve the liquid.

2 Preheat the oven to 350°. Thoroughly grease a deep 7 in round cake pan and line the base with nonstick baking paper.

3 Sift the flour into a bowl with the nutmeg. Stir in the brown sugar, fruit, and tea. Add the oil and milk and mix well.

4 Spoon the mixture into the prepared pan and sprinkle with raw sugar. Bake for 50–55 minutes or until firm. Turn out and cool on a wire rack.

SUNFLOWER-RAISIN SCONES

INGREDIENTS

Makes 10–12
2 cups self-rising flour
1 tsp baking powder
2 tbsp soft sunflower margarine
2 tbsp sugar
⅓ cup raisins
2 tbsp sunflower seeds
⅔ cup plain yogurt
about 2–3 tbsp skim milk

1 Preheat the oven to 450°F. Lightly oil a baking sheet. Sift the flour and baking powder into a bowl and rub in the margarine evenly.

2 Stir in the sugar, raisins, and half the sunflower seeds, then mix in the yogurt, with just enough milk to make a fairly soft, but not sticky dough.

3 Roll out on a lightly floured surface to about ¾ in thickness. Cut into 2½ in flower shapes or rounds with a cookie cutter and lift onto the baking sheet.

4 Brush with milk and sprinkle with the reserved sunflower seeds, then bake for 10–12 minutes, until puffed and golden brown.

5 Cool the scones on a wire rack. Serve split and spread with jam or low fat spread.

NUTRITION NOTES

Per portion:
Energy	176Kcals/742kJ
Fat	5.32g
Saturated fat	0.81g
Cholesterol	0.84mg
Fiber	1.26g

PRUNE AND CANDIED PEEL BUNS

INGREDIENTS

Makes 12
2 cups flour
2 tsp baking powder
⅔ cup raw sugar
½ cup chopped dried prunes
⅓ cup chopped candied citrus peel
finely grated rind of 1 lemon
¼ cup sunflower oil
5 tbsp skim milk

NUTRITION NOTES

Per portion:
Energy	135Kcals/570kJ
Fat	3.35g
Saturated fat	0.44g
Cholesterol	0.13mg
Fiber	0.86g

1 Preheat the oven to 400°F. Lightly oil a large baking sheet. Sift together the flour and baking powder, then stir in the sugar, prunes, peel, and lemon rind.

2 Mix the oil and milk, then stir into the mixture, to make a dough which just binds together.

3 Spoon coarse mounds onto the baking sheet and bake for 20 minutes, until golden. Cool on a wire rack.

INDEX